THE NEW RECEPTIONIST

An essential guide to the
professional workplace

HANNA SMITH

Published by The Hanna Smith Agency
Bloemfontein, South Africa
www.thehannasmithagency.com
Editor: Sheena Carnie
Paperback design and layout: Riaan Relihan
Cover photo by Joel Filipe on Unsplash

ISBN: 9781795640336

Disclaimer
Although the publisher has made every effort to ensure that the information in this book was correct at press time, the author and publisher do not assume and hereby disclaim any liability to any party for any loss, damage, or disruption caused by errors or omissions, whether such errors or omissions result from negligence, accident or any other cause.
Although every effort has been made to ensure web information and URLs were correct at time of publication, the author and publisher do not guarantee the availability and/or accuracy of any web-related information.
This book does not provide any legal advice whatsoever, and nothing in this book should be construed as such. This book should be used for information purposes only; it does not replace company policy, company preference or common sense.
The New Receptionist is an independent publication and is neither affiliated to, nor authorized, sponsored or approved by Microsoft Corporation or Adobe Systems Incorporated.

Figure 1 and *figure 2* are used with permission from Microsoft.

For my mother who raised two children on a secretary's salary, my sister who told me I should finish this book and publish it, and my husband who is always there to applaud completion of my crazy projects. This book is for all of you.

•

I would like to thank my husband, George Tsikkos, Regional Manager at LexisNexis® South Africa for his invaluable contributions to the subject matter selected for this book, Dr Damian Viviers from the Commercial Practice Group at Phatshoane Henney Attorneys for reviewing the chapter on POPI and the GDPR, and Bianca Cremer from CoetzeeSmit Chartered Accountants (SA) for her generous assistance.

Table of contents

Preface

If you have purchased this book you are probably starting a job at a reception desk or are thinking of applying for a position as a receptionist. Congratulations, the reception desk is a great place to start a career! Many successful people including Karen Kaplan (CEO of Hill Holliday) and celebrated literary agent, the late David Miller, started out as receptionists.

Who is this book for?

This book is for inexperienced receptionists and assistants who are beginning a career in a professional workplace, and anyone else who wants to learn more about the various topics the book covers.

Who is this book *not* for?

This book is an introduction to a professional environment and covers essential skills for those who are starting out as receptionists or assistants; it is not a manual for experienced executive and administrative assistants who are familiar with privacy laws, company structure and general essential skills.

Why did I write the book?

I feel there has been a gap between learning guides and the practice of working in a professional environment, and I hope this book will bridge that gap. In addition to being given tips on essential telephone and computer skills, in this book the new receptionist will learn about the professional environment and will be able to start his or her first day with confidence. The new receptionist will also learn what a COO is — along with other lingo they will hear in a business environment — and how data privacy laws affect the reception desk. My book covers these and other topics in an effort to guide new receptionists through their work space and typical daily duties.

I hope that reading this book helps to build your confidence, especially if you're preparing for your first day. I want you to walk into a new office and know how to handle angry callers, deal with privacy issues, not have to ask someone what a CTO is, and to say yes when a manager who you have just met asks if you can quickly take the minutes of a meeting.

I wish you success in your new job!

Hanna Smith
The Hanna Smith Agency
www.thehannasmithagency.com

Introduction

Most of us know how to use a computer, answer a telephone and write an email, but can we do it in a professional setting? *The New Receptionist* gives special attention to working in a professional business environment where you'll need to know what the GDPR and POPI are, what terms such as R&D and CRM are used for, and how to perform general essential tasks professionally.

The New Receptionist covers the following areas

Writing a CV and covering letter, the daily duties of most receptionists, including receiving guests, petty cash control, arranging courier services and business travel, working with different time zones, softphones and hardphones, answering the phones, transferring calls, taking messages, telephone etiquette, dealing with angry callers, handling business correspondence, terms used in a business environment, who is who in the company structure, POPI, managing your time, work, career and more.

How to use this book

Each chapter of *The New Receptionist* focuses on a specific topic; a summary at the beginning of each chapter provides a list of the topics in that section. **Notes** and **tips** are provided to clarify or offer additional information on a topic.

Terms for which additional explanation is required are listed under **Terms and Definitions** in each chapter. If you do not understand a term that is used in the chapter text, refer to the Terms and Definitions section. If the term is not available in the Terms and Definitions section, consult a reputable dictionary or ask the author to add it in a later edition at www.thehannasmithagency.com/books.

A connected world

The internet has opened communication pathways, broken boundaries between cultures and built a new kind of community — a connected, global community.

Global communities embrace diversity, accept change and welcome new ways of doing things, so *The New Receptionist* does not stipulate that one method of doing something is necessarily better than another, it merely provides one way to get you started. In a connected world where company offices span the globe, ways of doing things (even within the same company) might differ and you will have to adjust to that, but at least you will have a solid foundation to start with.

Chapter one
Writing a CV and covering letter

A Curriculum Vitae (CV) introduces a candidate to a potential employer. Where possible, register your CV with a reputable personnel agency. A good personnel agency will work with you on your CV and find the best company for you. Whether you are working with an agency or drafting a CV on your own, make sure it looks professional and contains all the relevant information.

Summary of what is included in this section:
- **Writing a CV**
- **Writing a covering letter**
- **Interview tips**

Note: The terms "CV" and "résumé" are often used interchangeably, particularly outside the US, however, there is a difference between the two. A résumé is a summary of your employment history while a CV is a longer document that provides the full details of the sections in your résumé. This section refers to writing a CV.

Writing a CV
Layout

Many companies offer a guideline for the layout and information they wish to see on a candidate's CV, or even a template the candidate may download and fill in. Most recruitment agencies offer templates or an online profile that constructs a CV from the information the candidate enters. If there is no guideline, template or online profile to work from, a typical CV is structured as follows:
- Personal information and contact information
- Employment history and areas of expertise

- Qualifications
- Awards and achievements
- Hobbies
- References

Tips on writing a CV

Separate sections of information in a logical way. At the top include your name, title, surname, professional title, age, driver's licence code, contact information and any other personal details the job advertisement asked for. Next, include your employment history and specific skills as well as degrees, diplomas, and certificates you've earned. End with awards, achievements, hobbies, and a reference.

Note: Check the advertisement carefully for any specific information that must be included in the CV.

Note: Use an email address that looks professional. Try to avoid using supersexy63567546325@somedomain.co.za as your email address in the contact section.

Less is more. If you can include all the information for each section of the CV in a neat and logical way and get it all to fit on three or four pages, you have written enough. Avoid repeating information or including irrelevant information to make your CV look longer.

When compiling a list of previous employers **start with the most recent** and work your way back. Always include your role at the company and the dates that you were employed. If you do not have any work experience that is okay, simply include any voluntary or community work, or projects you have participated in. Head that section **Community Work Experience and Projects** or something similar.

If you were previously employed, **include a list of specific duties and responsibilities** for each position held; it is important to show a potential employer what you did at your last job. If the list is not that long that is fine; do not make up activities just for the sake of it.

It is not always necessary to include a **reason for leaving** your last job unless it is significant in some way, such as your previous employer closing the business or the fact that you earned a degree and are looking for a job in line with your new skills. If a potential employer wants to know why you left your last job, he or she will ask you in an interview.

Highlight areas of expertise. If you are an expert at something that is relevant to the position you are applying for, include it in your CV. For instance, if you are an expert at using Microsoft® Word® then be sure to say so.

Use CV Assistant in Word (or Résumé Assistant, depending on where you are in the world). This feature is available to Office 365 subscribers and provides examples of how people describe their work experience on LinkedIn. The CV Assistant helps to define a list of skills that is relevant to your job role, all without you leaving Microsoft Word.

Include academic qualifications. Always add your academic qualifications and state the college or university name along with the year the qualification was completed.

Add a professional photo. If you include a photo make sure it is a professional photo; do not include photos that were taken on a night out or on vacation.

List any additional spoken and written languages. Speaking and writing multiple languages is highly beneficial in both multicultural communities and international settings.

Do not add random hobbies that are not relevant to the position you are applying for. Instead, add specific interests that are relevant to your personality. If you like to paint then tell the potential employer what kind of painting you like to do. For example, "I have a passion for capturing the South African landscape; my latest works show the effect of the drought on farms in the Western Cape."

It is not necessary to list more than one reference. If you are adding a reference, make sure it is someone who knows you well and who is from a professional or academic institution. Always inform the person that you are adding them as a reference.

Be truthful. Never provide information that is inaccurate or dishonest. For example, if you are in the process of applying for a driver's licence do not state that you already have one. Instead, state the date on which you hope to obtain your licence.

Spend time writing your CV. Your CV introduces you to a potential employer, and first impressions do count. Take time to draft, rewrite, and edit your CV. It is also a good idea to have someone else read it.

Proofread your CV. Never send out a CV that has not been proofread. Your CV is a good indication of the kind of work you will hand in on a daily basis and it will give a poor impression if there are mistakes in your CV.

Use standard fonts if you are applying to a traditional or corporate company. Fancy fonts can be difficult to read and are distracting. Calibri, Arial, and Times New Roman are best. Choose size 12 and apply a 1.5 line paragraph spacing. Make sure the font colour is black, and that headings are underlined or bold. Yellow, orange, pink and green text is especially difficult to read.

Number the pages of your CV. In Word, select **Insert > Page Number.** From the dropdown menu choose how you would like the number to display on the page.

Make use of templates. If you do not know how to structure your CV ask a recruitment agency for a template. If you are applying to a specific company, check their website for online CV templates and advice on applying to the company.

Follow the rules stipulated in the advert for uploading and emailing CVs. Companies might have specific rules for uploading CVs to their database or for emailing CVs to a department or person. Check the file format that is required, whether they require a photo, and the size limit of the file. If you do not follow the submission guidelines your CV will most likely be rejected by the server or deleted by the person who receives it. Unless otherwise instructed, upload your CV as a PDF file. To save your CV as a PDF from Word, select **File** > **Save As** > *Browse to the location* > *Give your file a name* > select **PDF** (*.PDF) in the **Save as type** dropdown field and select **Save**.

If you are uploading your CV to a company's website, or are emailing your CV to a specific department or person, **make sure you follow the naming convention** if one is indicated. If there is no specific instruction on how the CV must be named, use your surname and initials, and the position you are applying for as the file name; for example, Jones P - Reception CV.PDF. If you have to email your CV some companies might ask you to include certain information in the subject line of the email, such as your full name, the name of the position, or the reference number of the job that was advertised.

Check your CV extremely carefully if you are sending it to more than one company. I cannot stress this enough – if you are editing a template of your CV make sure that you address the covering letter to the correct company or person!

Writing a covering letter

A covering letter is a brief statement of why you are applying for the position and what your career goals are. A covering letter (or cover letter) accompanies a CV and is usually written in the first person, so use "I" instead of "she" or "he".

Tips on writing a covering letter

Do not repeat what is in your CV. Repeating information will make the CV longer than it has to be. A cover letter is an introduction, it is not a list of your qualifications or work experience.

Tailor each cover letter to the company you are applying to. Make sure you research the company and address the letter to the correct person.

Start with the **reason you are applying for the job**, and mention if you are responding to a job advertisement. Where possible address the letter to a specific person, usually the person who posted the job advertisement or the person listed as the contact.

For example:

Dear Ms Watson

I am writing in response to the position advertised on 12 July 2019 on the vacancies page of your website. The reference number is A23421.

Follow the requirements for the cover letter. Sometimes companies will ask for specific details to be included in the cover letter, so make sure you put these in the body of the letter.

Include why you are applying for the position that was advertised and why you will be a good fit for the company. Demonstrate an interest in the company but only add details that are relevant to the position.

For example:

I have recently completed a BA degree in Creative Writing at the University of the Free State and am looking for a position in the publishing industry. I am currently employed as a sales consultant at the university's book shop.

I have read many of your non-fiction titles, and especially enjoy those from Jennifer Jones and Brad Cooper. I wrote an essay on Jones' cookbook *We are Vegan Friendly* in 2018 and the essay won The Hanna Smith 2018 student essay competition.

Or

Willow Books specialises in fantasy fiction which is a genre that I particularly enjoy. In 2018 I wrote an essay on Jenny Smith's fantasy worlds and the essay won The Hanna Smith 2018 essay competition.

Express some interest in an interview. Let the company know when you are available for interviews and how they can contact you.
For example:
I am available between 13:00 and 17:00 on weekdays. If you prefer to contact me via email, my email address is belinda@theuniversity.co.za.
I am looking forward to hearing from you.

Yours sincerely,
Belinda Jones

Unless the company asks for the cover letter and the CV as **two separate documents**, insert the cover letter at the front of the CV and upload it all as one file.

Interview tips
Interviews can be conducted face-to-face or online. Online interviews are conducted when the interviewer is located in a different city or country to the candidate, or when an online interview is convenient for some other reason. This section provides tips for both face-to-face and online interviews.
Interviews can differ considerably from company to company, but there are a few general guidelines that will help you prepare for an interview.

Face-to-face interviews

Be on time. Never be late for an interview. Check the address and make sure you know how to get there. If you are running late for an acceptable reason (such as a traffic accident or an unforeseeable weather change), call the company and ask if you may arrive late or if they are willing to reschedule the interview.

Dress appropriately. Dress neatly and wear a jacket; avoid flamboyant jewellery and accessories. Dressing up for an interview shows that you have respect for the process and for the interviewers.

Think about your perfume. Avoid strong perfume or cologne, or hair and skin products that have a strong smell. On the other hand, a subtle, clean fragrance is pleasant and professional.

Turn off your phone. Never answer your phone or use your phone during an interview unless the interviewer asks you to do so for some reason.

Take along a notebook and a pen. It is always a good idea to take a notebook and a pen to an interview; having something to write on makes you look and feel prepared.

Take along a copy of your CV. Print at least two copies of your CV in case the interviewer does not have a copy on hand or has asked another employee to join the interview at the last minute. A copy of your CV is also useful when the interviewer refers to a section that you may need to clarify. Read the section before you answer unless you are confident you know exactly what you wrote word for word.

Research the company. Always familiarise yourself with the company before the interview so that you are prepared for any company-specific questions, or for the "Why do you want to work for us?" question. You cannot answer this question if you do not know what the company does.

Be prepared to answer a variety of questions. Interviewers have different styles; some will ask general questions while others will focus on specific skills. In general, be prepared to answer a variety of questions, such as versions of any of the following (amongst many other questions an interviewer might ask):

What are your strengths and weaknesses?
Why would you like to work for us?
Why should we choose you?
What are your short term and long term goals?
How would you describe your personality?
Do you perform well under stress?
Describe a stressful situation and how you handled it.
How do you deal with conflict?
Give an example of how you dealt with conflict in the past.
Do you prefer to work in a team or on your own, and why?
Describe a time when you prepared for a specific task and the task changed at the last minute. What was the outcome, and how did you feel about performing the new task?
Tell us about a time when nothing went your way, and how you dealt with it.
What are you passionate about?
What are your salary expectations?

Do not interrupt the interviewer. Wait for the interviewer to finishing speaking before you speak.

If you do not understand a question, politely say so. No one will bite your head off because you did not understand a question. It is also okay to clarify the question before you answer by asking, for example, "Would you like me to describe the process I applied or just the outcome?"

Prepare a list of questions of your own. An interviewer might ask if you have any questions for them.

Express an interest in working at the company at the end of the interview. Without sounding pushy, mention, for example, that you would be thrilled to work for the company, or that you would enjoy working in the industry.

Confirm the next step. Confirming the next step shows that you are interested in working for the company, and that you are organised.

Make sure you remember the interviewer's name. Remembering the interviewer's name will help you if you need to send through further information or documents after the interview. If you're asked to send information to the interviewer, in your notebook write down the details of what you need to send and how you should send it to make sure you don't make any mistakes.

Thank the interviewers. It is good manners to thank the interviewers for asking you to meet with them, and for their time.

Online interviews
Most of the tips for face-to-face interviews also apply to online interviews; however, online interviews can be challenging as certain technical aspects need to be considered.

Tips for a successful online interview:
Check that your connection to the internet is working. Make sure you can connect to a stable internet connection for the duration of your online interview.

Check that the software program is working. If you are using a software communication program like Skype, open the program and log in to check that everything is working correctly well before the start time of your interview. If the company sends you a link for a web meeting in an email, the email should contain instructions for logging on to a website. Read through the instructions in the email and make sure you understand how to log on to the website and what internet browser you should use.

Check that the computer's camera and microphone are working. Ask a friend to call you so that you have an opportunity to test the computer's microphone and camera.

Make sure the camera frames your head and shoulders in the middle of the screen. Try to avoid being too close to the camera or too far away.

Use a room that is quiet. Avoid sitting in an area that is noisy or distracting.

If you are at home or at a friend's home, **tell them that you are in a job interview** and ask not to be disturbed.

Check that the room is well lit and that you display well on the screen.

Check that the room's background is appropriate. Remove busy posters and distracting objects from the background. Keep the background simple and make sure it looks clean.

Make allowances for IT issues. If you experience technical difficulties during the interview ask for a few minutes to rectify the issue. If you are not IT savvy ask a friend who is good with computers to be on standby during your interview.

If the interviewer is experiencing technical difficulties be patient, stay available at the screen, and wait for them to make a decision to proceed with the interview or not.

Terms and Definitions

CV: Curriculum vitae is a Latin expression that means "course of life". It is used to describe the course of one's career.

IT savvy: A person is IT savvy when they have above-average knowledge of how computers, computer networks and applications work.

Chapter two
Daily tasks

Starting a new job is stressful; lack of experience, lack of training and long periods of unemployment often contribute to the stress one feels leading up to that first day. The good news is that a position at the reception desk is a great start to building your career. Whether you are just entering the job market or are transferring to the corporate world, you have made a great decision. Some receptionists love the work so much they make it a career, so gear up, kick the stress, and get ready for a wonderful journey.

Summary of what is included in this section:
- **Getting started**
- **Receiving guests**
- **Dealing with petty cash**
- **Using courier services**
- **Arranging travel for the purpose of business**
- **A checklist for meetings**

Your first day can be overwhelming. The job is new, the people are new and the industry is new, but don't panic. Yes, you have to learn a few things, but chances are you don't have to do it on your own; in most cases someone will be available to train you.

Tip: If no one is available to assist you on your first day, ask the person who made the introductions who you should refer your questions to. Companies don't always have everything figured out, and will welcome some interaction from you.

Tip: Have a notebook you can easily carry around and a pen or pencil ready for taking notes (a tablet will also work). In fact, always have a notebook handy; a receptionist is everyone's assistant.

Your instructor will no doubt show you the reception desk. If you already have experience working in an office then most of the technical items listed here will be familiar to you, but if you are new at the reception desk this section will help you get started.

Getting started
Equipment that might be located at the reception desk
<u>Printers and scanners</u>
Printers and scanners are usually shared by employees because they are expensive and are often misused when not monitored. Typically, a printer, scanner, or printer/scanner combo is connected to the network (this allows everyone in the office to print or scan regardless of where they sit) and is often physically located at the reception desk. Printers and scanners can also be located in a designated printing room or office. Some staff members, like the accountant who keeps confidential company information, have printers installed in their private offices. If there is a printer, scanner, or printer/scanner combo at the reception desk, ask if you are required to assist staff with printing and scanning.

Tip: If you *are* required to print or scan documents on behalf of other employees, ask for a quick demonstration. Print and scan a piece of scrap paper and note the procedure in your notebook. It is advisable to learn how to operate the printers and scanners early; don't leave this step to when the CEO needs a document printed or scanned in a hurry.

<u>Computer</u>
There is a very good chance that you will have a computer at your desk. At reception the tasks to be performed on the computer can include any of the following: phone system management, drafting letters and emails, drafting spreadsheets, transcription, internet research, messaging, stock

management, invoicing, taking note of surveillance footage from cameras located around the office or at the front door, access to specialised software programs, and much more. However, before you jump in, take note of whether you need a password to access the computer. If your company has an IT Department they might have set up a user profile on your computer. In some cases the IT Department might not have given you the password to your profile on your first day, so if your computer asks for a password and you have not been given one, check in with the IT Department.

Note: If your company has an IT Department, your user profile, email and email signature, software programs the company requires you to use, and so on, might be ready for you from day one. If you need assistance with your computer ask for the IT Department's telephone number or extension and let them know you need their assistance. If your company outsources their IT, ask for assistance internally before making any support requests. IT companies apply charges to support requests, and some might even require a reference number from your company in order to assist you.

Telephone

Nowadays telephones come in a variety of forms; the reception desk might have a traditional hardphone that sits on your desk, a softphone that is installed on your computer, or both. A softphone requires a headset or similar device that is connected to the computer or telephone system. Since answering the phones is a crucial part of a receptionist's job, explaining how the phones work should be your instructor's top priority. Make sure you take detailed notes of how the phones work, and how to answer, transfer, return, and end calls properly. Chapter three focuses specifically on answering phones and telephone etiquette.

Transcription devices

Dictaphones and transcription devices convert recorded voice files into text on a computer. Dictaphones are useful for capturing the minutes of a meeting, on-the-go notes, reports, ideas, letters, and even entire books. On the other hand, transcription devices are useful for converting the captured voice files to text. The process of turning the recorded material into text is called *transcription.*

Transcription devices come in all shapes and sizes. Some devices are simple, and others come in kits that contain foot controls, headsets, and software. If the reception desk has a transcription device, ask for a quick demonstration and note the procedure in your notebook. If the device is linked to a specific software program, ask someone to go through the essentials of the program with you.

Note: Word 2019 has a **Dictate** function on the **Home** tab (see Chapter seven for the location of the **Home** tab) that converts spoken words to text. To use the **Dictate** function a working microphone must be installed on your computer.

Tablets

Tablets are quickly becoming an essential part of every business. The benefits of these computer devices are that they're lightweight, relatively inexpensive, mobile, and easy to use. Most software programs can now be replaced by a simple app on your tablet. In the receptionist's field a tablet can be used for booking stock in and out, making all kinds of reservations, updating the company's social media pages, filling in forms, managing calendars, accessing internal documents or learning material, logging onto the company's customer relationship manager (CRM) system, tracking vehicles in the field, submitting claims, taking notes, and much more.

Receiving guests

Receiving guests is high on the list of duties for most receptionists. When clients enter the reception area make sure they know exactly where to go or where to wait. Smile and make them feel comfortable at all times.

If you are receiving a large number of guests simultaneously and they will be required to wait, make sure there is adequate seating before the time of arrival. You don't want to be running up and down looking for chairs in front of any guests.

If you are required to show guests to another room, make sure that the reception area is not left unattended while you do so. If the waiting room is on another floor of the building or down a long hallway, ask a member of staff for assistance beforehand. New guests should never enter a reception area that is unattended as they might wander to private "employees only" areas looking for someone to assist them; nor should they be left waiting outside a building entrance because there is no one to buzz them in.

If guests need a name badge for an event or conference, ensure that each person's title, name, surname, designation and company name are correct. Most executives (if not all) will not simply scratch out a company name that is incorrect so that they can wear their name badge, especially if the incorrect company name is that of a competitor. If you're unsure if all your information is correct, call the guest's company and ask for details from a personal assistant or check the guest's company's website. If, however, you find out at the last minute that something on the name badge is incorrect, print another at the soonest opportunity and discreetly offer it to the person during a break. Unless it is absolutely necessary, avoid writing on a name badge with a pen as it looks unprofessional.

Note: Try to secure the name badges to lanyards. Badges that must be pinned to clothing are not ideal because a name badge on a dress or shirt can easily be covered by a jacket, whereas a name badge on a lanyard is visible at all times.

Note: If you are catering for guests find out if anyone requires a special meal (e.g. vegetarian or halaal) or if anyone has any allergies. Nowadays, special meals are easily available from supermarkets and restaurants. If for some reason you are not able to provide a special meal, inform the guest prior to their arrival. If they bring their own food then offer to heat it up (if necessary) and offer them clean cutlery to use.

Dealing with petty cash

Petty cash is a specific amount of cash money that is used for small, ad hoc office expenses such as stationery, tips, small catering expenses, printing and binding, and so on. As employees use money from the petty cash fund the fund is replenished, usually weekly, bi-monthly or monthly. A designated person will control the petty cash.

Tips for working with petty cash
Keep records. Always make sure that every withdrawal from the petty cash fund is recorded on a log or spreadsheet. Microsoft Excel® is a handy application for creating spreadsheets.

Use a petty cash receipt book. Each time money leaves the fund the person requesting a withdrawal must sign a receipt (a receipt is also known as a petty cash voucher). Their name, the amount they are withdrawing, and the purpose of the withdrawal must be noted. Do not leave this step for later in the day as you might get busy and forget to do it.

Request a purchase receipt. When at all possible, request a purchase receipt for any items or services purchased. A receipt also makes it easier to balance change returned to the petty cash box.

Never leave the petty cash lying around. Petty cash can disappear faster than you think so never leave money lying around. If you are responsible for the petty cash, keep it locked away. Make sure that the keys to the money tin or the safe where the petty cash is stored are secured and only accessible to authorized persons.

Note: Petty cash is also sometimes known as the cash float.

Petty cash reconciliation
A petty cash reconciliation is a document that shows the total receipts (disbursements or money paid out), purpose of expenditure, and amount reimbursed to petty cash (the amount that the petty cash must be paid back). For example, if the petty cash float is R1000.00 and the total receipts equal R700.00 then the petty cash must be reimbursed with R700.00. Example of a petty cash reconciliation:

Petty Cash Reconciliation
November 2019

Date	Receipt	Account Code	Debit	Credit	Balance	Signature
						Cash float: R 1000.00
02/11/2019	HS143	TRV901	258.00		742.00	Joe Big
07/11/2019	HS144	STA345	54.50		687.50	Mark May
08/11/2019	HS145	TRV901	350.00		337.50	Sally Peters
20/11/2019	HS146	CAT020	87.00		250.50	Joe Jones
22/11/2019	HS147	STA345	65.00		185.50	Jane Su

Total Receipts:	R814.50
Less cash float:	R185.50

Amount Requested: R 814.50

Date: _____

Authorized signature: _____

If the petty cash reconciliation shows money is left over (i.e. there is more money than what there should be), note the amount that is over on the reconciliation form. Place the amount of cash that is over in a small bank bag or envelope, and store it in the money tin or safe where the petty cash is stored. Investigate money that is over and write down your findings on the bag or envelope (e.g. R5.60 over: incorrect change given on receipt HS324). If there is money missing (i.e. there is less than there should be), investigate the missing amount of money and note it on the reconciliation form. If money is missing it should be reported immediately.

Using courier services

Courier services are faster and more reliable than state owned postal services because they are usually privately owned. Postal services that send regular mail are generally cheaper than privately owned courier services;

however, for the purpose of business, a courier service is preferred because couriers offer more benefits and a wider range of options.

Note: Regular mail is also known as snail mail.

Benefits of choosing a courier service for documents and parcels
A courier service usually offers **same-day delivery**, next day delivery, and express delivery for time-critical parcels.
Courier services offer **door-to-door delivery.** This is useful when sending confidential or sensitive documents.
Courier companies offer **accounts** (the company settles the account at the end of the month) which speeds up the process of booking a collection.
Courier companies offer a **pick-up service.** If you send parcels with the public postal service you have to drive there and stand in a queue.
Most courier companies offer an **online booking service**. You will use a username and password to access your online account. Parcels sent via an online booking system usually have more tracking options.
Some courier companies offer **packaging assistance.**

Tips for sending documents and parcels with a courier service
Always **check that the recipient's name and title are correct.** If you are unsure of how to spell the recipient's name check on their company's website if they are listed, call the company's reception desk, or speak with an assistant. If the recipient is a woman and you are unsure of whether her title is Mrs or Miss, use Ms.

Always check that the recipient's **contact details** are correct. When possible include a telephone number for the recipient and check if a delivery note (a special delivery request) must be attached.

If you are sending a document or parcel to a company, **clearly indicate the name of the recipient** and their department so that the person who signs for the parcel knows exactly who to give it to. If a parcel is addressed to no one in particular, there is a good chance that no one will open it, or that it will be sent back.

Pack your parcel before scheduling a pickup because most couriers work with time-demanding schedules. It is also nerve-racking to pack a parcel while the delivery van is waiting for you.

Have all the documents ready in good time. If you need to fill out a form or prepare a commercial invoice for an international export parcel, make sure these are ready and signed by the appropriate parties before the courier arrives.

Note: A commercial invoice is a customs document that is used to declare the value and nature of items that are exported. These documents have a specific format but most courier companies have online templates that you may download, or an online form that will generate an invoice for you.

Take note of any prohibited items and other restrictions when sending items with couriers. Most couriers provide a list of prohibited items for each country, along with a list of items they will not import or export. Check the courier's website before sending items overseas.

If you are sending a stack of documents, **make sure they are secured** in sections with staples or elastic bands. Documents that cannot be stapled should be placed in envelopes. If you are sending a large number of documents in one document parcel or bag, separate documents into different envelopes and place the individual envelopes in the bag. Always remember to write the name of the document on the envelope, e.g., J Jones non-disclosure agreement, or P Smith work for hire contract.

Always have packaging material available at the office as this will save time when a parcel must be sent in a hurry. Most courier companies offer online purchasing options.

Always provide a **return address** so that undelivered parcels are returned to you.

Follow the courier's **packing advice** before sending parcels as some couriers have specific rules for packing certain items. If you do not follow the rules you may have to repack parcels at the last minute.

Note: Some couriers offer advice and tips on packing electronics, large parcels and even fashion and temperature sensitive items. Look for advice on weighing parcels, packing liquids and fragile items, considering the value of items, choosing packing materials, packing techniques, sealing and labelling.

Get a quotation. If your company needs a quote before booking a collection, visit the courier company's website for an online quote that you can print or email. If an online quotation service is not available, call the courier company and speak with a consultant.

Check if you need to add an **insurance option** to your shipment. Courier companies have different insurance options, such as once-off insurance for a particular shipment, or an insurance option that covers a range of shipments over a period of time.

Use the correct country code and postal code
Whether you are using a courier service or the public postal service, always check that you have entered the correct postal code or country code (when sending parcels internationally). If you are unsure of the code you must use, check online for a list; many courier services provide a list of country codes and postcode formats on their website. Always check codes from a reputable source.

Distributing post and parcels
A receptionist is often the person responsible for distributing incoming mail. Try to sort mail items before distributing them and check if any are

marked urgent. Urgent items should be delivered immediately, and regular items should be distributed at the same time each day.

Arranging travel for the purpose of business

Business travel covers any trips during which an employee will be representing the company. Business travel arrangements include booking hotels, flights and rental cars. When possible, work with a travel agent. Travel agencies offer all-inclusive packages and are useful when bookings need to be changed in a hurry or after hours.

Online booking on the company's website or portal

Some companies have an online system for booking travel. The purpose of such a system is to consolidate and control the fees, frequency, and procedures for travel. A company might have an account with a particular agency that offers discounts and packages, or a system that logs travel expenses in one program.

Whether you are booking on a company system, through an agent or online, here are a few tips for booking business travel for executives and senior staff.

Tips for booking hotels

Book a hotel that is **close to the venue where their conference or meeting is being held.** When executives travel they do not want to drive kilometres to attend meetings or events. If possible, book executives into the same hotel where their meeting or event is being held.

Tip: Some events have a special mailing list or secure event login on registration where special deals, parking vouchers and transport are advertised or arranged.

Find out from the staff member who's travelling if they require **specific amenities** at the hotel. Some executives like to stick to a routine even when travelling, such as attending a gym in the morning.

Before making the booking find out if a **bath or a shower is preferred.**

Some executives prefer a shower to a bath, or vice versa, for medical or other reasons.

A good breakfast can be a lifesaver for executives who have demanding schedules. Find out if the hotel must **cater for breakfast** and if there are any **special meal requirements.** If a special meal is required always confirm the request with the hotel.

Tips for booking a rental car
When booking a rental car, it is always a good idea to **include a GPS** if one is not already built into the car.

If executives are travelling with large items or big suitcases, **book a car that has a large boot** so that they do not have to place their personal luggage or valuable items on the back seat of the car. A large boot is also convenient for staff who have to travel with marketing banners and company stock.

Find out **what kind of car is required**; some executives like to drive luxury cars while others prefer vans or smaller cars.

Find out if you are required to include the **insurance option** on rental car bookings.
If a credit card needs to be presented when the car is collected from the rental agency, inform the driver so that he or she has the correct card available.

Find out if you must **book a chauffeur** to get the staff member to the airport. Some executives prefer to use a chauffeur service or an airport transfer service rather than driving a car to and from the airport. Both transport services and chauffeur services must be booked in advance.

Tips for booking air travel
Executives often travel both internationally and locally, and some executives travel almost every day of the week. Air travel can be exhaustive, so **make**

sure that all travel bookings are confirmed and well planned.

Ensure that the appropriate class has been booked. Although many companies allow business class travel, some do not. Class options that are typically available on most airlines are economy class, first class, and business class. Business class offers more amenities, luxury seating, preferential boarding and a better overall experience, but this option is very expensive. Economy class is a cheaper option used by most travellers.

Note the airline's rules for hand luggage and checked baggage. Different airlines and classes have different rules about the luggage weight, dimensions, and number of luggage items allowed. Hand luggage is taken on the plane and is placed in an overhead compartment during the flight. There are specific regulations for hand luggage including that most airlines do not allow liquids in containers of more than 100ml in volume.

Checked baggage is the suitcase that is checked-in and placed in a separate secured area in the plane. There are also specific rules and regulations for checked baggage. If executives are carrying items that do not fit the hand luggage or checked baggage specifications take note of the fees and conditions for excess baggage before booking the ticket, especially when there is a connecting flight as the other airline might not have the same rules or rates for excess baggage.

Note: If you are taking a connecting flight it means that you are flying to the destination on more than one plane and you will have a stop over in a city on the way to switch planes.

Tip: Where possible book a direct flight, or connecting flights within a few hours of each other; executives do not want to spend days in an airport waiting for their next flight.

Ensure that flights are booked with the **proper meal requirements** if there are any.

Print hotel and car vouchers, directions to hotels and meetings along with airline tickets and specific airline rules. Where possible include GPS coordinates of the venues. Place the information in a folder or envelope and include a neatly printed summary of hotel book-in and book-out times, and check-in times for flights. If you are sending an email to the executive regarding the details of the trip, attach the information to one email and include a summary in the body of the email. Always include the name and contact number of the travel agent or person who booked the tickets in case arrangements need to be changed or flights are delayed or cancelled.

Note: At this point it will be clear that you need to ask a lot of questions in the beginning. As you get to know everyone's preferences and become familiar with the events and meetings they typically attend, booking travel gets easier. If executives have their own personal assistants there is a good chance that you will not be required to book travel, but personal assistants take leave and fall ill, and as the receptionist you will be the backup.

Working with time zones

Time zones are confusing to first time assistants who are arranging international travel. To keep things simple, a time zone is the local time of a country or a region. On the other hand, UTC (Coordinated Universal Time) is a world time standard that is written UTC+ or UTC- to indicate the region's difference from UTC. For example, South African Standard Time (SAST) is UTC +2. This means that the SAST time zone is two hours ahead of UTC. Eastern European Time (EET) and Israel Standard Time (IST) are in the same time zone as SAST – UTC +2. UTC shares the same time as Greenwich Mean Time (GMT).

Note: Daylight Saving Time (DST) is when the clock is moved forward by one hour from standard time in the spring, and back again to standard time in the autumn. Daylight Saving Time was established to make better use of daylight. The United Kingdom, most locations in the United States, Cyprus, Bulgaria and Germany are a few of the countries around the world that observed DST in 2018. For a full list of countries that observe DST, visit Time and Date at https://www.timeanddate.com/time/dst/2018.html.

Common time zones

ACT: Australian Central Time
          – Australia: UTC +9:30 / +10:30

BST: British Summer Time
          – Europe: UTC +1

CAT: Central African Time
          – Africa: UTC +2

CET: Central European Time
          – Europe, Africa: UTC +1

CST: China Standard Time
          – Asia: UTC +8

EDT: Eastern Daylight Time
          – North America, Caribbean: UTC -4

EST: Eastern Standard Time
          – North America, Caribbean, Central America: UTC -5

GMT: Greenwich Mean Time
          – Europe, Africa, North America, Antarctica: UTC +0

IST: India Standard Time
          – Asia: UTC +5:30

PST: Pacific Standard Time
          – North America: UTC -8

SAST: South African Standard Time
          – Africa: UTC +2

If UTC is 19:00, it is 15:00 in New York (EDT is UTC -4), and 20:00 in London (BST is UTC +1).

Note: Some time zones have the same abbreviations as others, for example, BST is the abbreviation for British Summer Time, Bangladesh Standard Time, and Bougainville Standard Time.

Note: Time and Date AS is an excellent resource for assistants arranging international travel. The website includes a Time Zone Converter and a World Clock. Visit Time and Date at https://www.timeanddate.com.

A checklist for meetings

Arranging meetings can be stressful for the new receptionist, especially because no two meetings are the same. Meetings come in all types and sizes; they can be conducted in an office between two or more persons, or can be held at venues with multiple attendees.

If you are arranging a meeting at a venue where multiple attendees will be present, the following checklist will help you get started:

✓ Confirm the time, date and venue of the meeting with all the attendees and the person you're liaising with at the venue.

✓ Make a note of the names of the attendees and present it to the person hosting the meeting along with any additional information they have asked for. Make sure you do this well before the start of the meeting.

Always ask the following:

✓ Must I print an attendance register?

✓ Must I print and bind documentation for each attendee?

✓ Must stationery be available?

✓ Do the attendees require name badges?

✓ Does the host require a projector?

✓ Must there be an internet connection available?

✓ Must I book a sound engineer or does the venue have an in-house engineer and sound equipment available?

✓ Must I arrange refreshments or snacks?

✓ If so, what time must refreshments and snacks be served?

✓ Do any of the attendees require transport to and from the meeting, and who is responsible for arranging that transport?

✓ Do the attendees require a special pass or access code to enter the venue where the meeting is being held?

✓ Does the venue offer secure parking?

✓ Do any of the attendees require a hotel booking, and who is responsible for making those bookings?

Terms and Definitions

Amenities: Features and facilities like a gym, pool, spa and laundry service that a hotel has available for guests.

App: An application (software) that is downloaded to a mobile device. There is an app for almost anything these days, such as for playing games, learning languages, tracking your fitness, listening to music, writing, and much more.

Dictaphone: Digital voice recorder.

Direct flight: A flight between two points which usually includes a stop somewhere, but the passengers stay on the plane during the stop and proceed to the destination without changing flight numbers or planes.

GPS: A Global Positioning System (GPS) unit uses a satellite network to pinpoint a specific location. In a car a GPS is used for navigation.

Host: The person or organisation arranging the meeting.

IT: Information Technology (IT) includes anything to do with computers, networks, telecommunications, software, hardware, and the internet.

In-house: If something is done "in-house" it means that it is done for the company by the company's employees.

Network printer: A printer that is connected to a network and is shared by the employees.

Tablet: A tablet, also called a tablet computer, is a mobile device that can perform most of the functions of a traditional computer.

Chapter three

The telephone and telephone etiquette

A receptionist is usually a person's first point of contact with a company, and the receptionist's level of professionalism is a reflection of the professionalism of the entire company.

Summary of what is included in this section:
· **Reception matters**
· **Answering the phone, transferring calls, and taking messages**
· **Telephone etiquette**
· **Dealing with angry customers**
· **Two scenarios and how to handle them**

Reception matters

As a receptionist your first task, and in some cases your only task, is to answer the phone. If a receptionist does not transfer calls correctly, takes incorrect messages, or is irritable and unprofessional, the caller will assume that the entire company is disorganised and unprofessional.

Within the company, a receptionist who is able to screen and transfer calls, take detailed messages, handle difficult callers with ease, and convey a professional tone, is valued as an integral part of the team.

Note: Some companies have more than one receptionist and they each have their own specific list of duties. Answering the phone and taking messages will likely be a task assigned to both receptionists.

Answering the phone, transferring calls, and taking messages

To answer the phone, transfer calls, and take messages, you need to establish the following:

The physical location of the phone

If you do not see a traditional telephone or hardphone on the desk, look for a headset. If the company is using softphones, you will answer the phone from a program that is installed on a computer.

Note: A **hardphone** looks and operates much like a traditional telephone. The difference between a hardphone and a traditional telephone is that a hardphone is internet based (it plugs into an IP network), whereas a traditional telephone plugs into a copper line infrastructure. Traditional copper line phones are often referred to as landlines.

Note: A **softphone** is a software program that acts like a phone. A softphone is internet based and runs on most smartphones, computers and tablets. When telephone calls are made over the internet they are called VoIP calls.

How do I answer the phone?

Here I'm referring to the words you use when you answer an incoming call. If the company prefers a phrase that includes the entire company name or department the caller has reached, answer the phone with the phrase, "Welcome to [the company name and department]. How may I direct your call?"

Some companies prefer a shorter phrase, such as "[The company name], good day."

It's a good idea to find this out right from the beginning.

How do I take a message?

Some companies have a paper based system for messages while others have an electronic system. Establish which you are required to use, and follow the instructions you are given. Make notes in your notebook of specific instructions.

Whether you are writing the message down on paper or typing the details on an electronic system (such as email or a message program of some sort), note the name of the person calling, their contact number, the company they are calling from (if applicable), the time of the call, and the message. If you are unable to get all these details immediately, write the name of the person and their contact number first as these details are important in order for them to receive a call back. Do not simply write "Anna called" as Anna could be anyone from anywhere.

Tip: If a caller returns a greeting, they will often tell you their name. Keep a scrap piece of paper and a pen handy and note the name and any other important information, such as a company name, from the start. If you need to take a message or resume the call (take the call back), remembering the caller's name shows that you have paid attention to their call. You don't want to ask someone for their name when they have already told you what it is.

Software based systems are handy for gathering a caller's information. Some systems retrieve an incoming caller's name and number from a pre-installed electronic phonebook. If you missed the caller's details because it was your very first unsupervised call, or the caller was in a rush and forgot to tell you their name or company name, relax. Look on the computer screen that has the applicable software running for a **History** or **Call History** list. If you are using a hardphone, look for a **History** button (also known as a soft key) on the phone itself. If you cannot retrieve any contact details from a history list, inform a manager or your instructor. If a history feature is not available for some reason, or the call displays without caller ID information, brush it off because we all make mistakes when we are new at things. Note your error and ensure you are able to perform the task of gathering a caller's details and their message next time.

How do I transfer calls?
Be sure to write down the instructions for transferring calls. Everyone requires some training when using softphones and even traditional switchboard-type phones.

There are two types of transfers – **cold transfers** (also known as blind transfers) and **warm transfers** (also known as attended transfers). Some companies prefer that incoming calls are screened before they are transferred to staff. Announcing who the caller is and what the purpose of the call is, is known as a warm transfer. The advantage of a warm transfer is that the recipient of the call has the opportunity to decide if they would like to speak with the caller or not. If the first recipient is not the correct person to handle the call, the receptionist has the opportunity to find the correct person in the company without transferring the caller back and forth. This saves the caller the frustration of speaking with the wrong person at the company. Screening calls is also important when executives do not want to speak to sales persons or callers who will waste their time. Personal assistants to executives will usually handle calls on their behalf. For this reason personal assistants and executive assistants are often called *gatekeepers* because they ultimately decide whether a caller may be transferred, or if the caller must leave a message or send their request in writing.

A cold or blind transfer occurs when a call is transferred to a callee without notifying the callee of the purpose of the call or the caller's name.

Note: When performing a warm transfer, if the caller did not provide their name or company name when asked, inform the recipient that the caller prefers not to identify himself or herself. The recipient will then have the opportunity to accept or decline the call.

Note: Never give out the personal contact information (or any information for that matter) of any staff member unless you have been given permission to do so. Giving out information could violate certain privacy laws or company policies on privacy.

Telephone etiquette
Learn the business
If you are entering an industry of which you have very little or no knowledge, learn as much as you can about the products, services, and the professional team at the company. Most companies have up-to-date websites with information on the product offerings, team members, services, and

geographical location of other offices. Familiarising yourself with the company's divisions and products or services will prepare you for basic questions a caller might ask, such as whether they have reached the correct office, or whether the company provides a specific service or product.

Calling persons on behalf of someone else

If a manager or executive asks you to set up a meeting but does not provide you with detailed information for that meeting, before you make the call think about some questions the person you are contacting to set the meeting with might ask. Think about questions like, "Should I prepare the conference room?", "Who is required to attend the meeting?" or "How much time should I book for the meeting?" You do not want to say, "I don't know" at every turn of the conversation. Try to gather as much information as possible before making the call and research phrases and terms you are not familiar with. For example, you might have to tell someone: "Mrs June would like to meet with you on Friday at nine to discuss the points the attorney raised in the non-disclosure agreement." If you know what a *non-disclosure agreement* is (and that it is sometimes referred to as an NDA) you will be more confident during the call.

Note: If you are setting up a meeting, always ascertain how many people will be attending the meeting so that the person responsible for arranging the gathering knows how many to prepare for. Always check whether a projector will be used during the meeting and who is responsible for setting it up.

Delivering a message on someone else's behalf

If you need to deliver a message on someone else's behalf and you do not have any information other than what you were told to say, clearly indicate that you are simply delivering a message.

For example, "I am delivering a message for Mr Jones from Country Estates. He will be at the corner of Eek and Bradbury at nine-thirty with the mock-up." If any questions arise it is acceptable to respond, "Mr Jones has not mentioned anything further in his message." The person will understand that you are simply the bearer of a message.

Tip: If you feel that a message's content is too technical or specialised for you to properly deliver, ask a colleague for assistance.

Never answer the phone when you are eating

The sound of chewing is unprofessional and unmannered, so avoid answering the phone when you are eating. If you are not able to swallow food safely before you answer the phone, transfer the call to a colleague who may assist with answering the phones, according to your company's policy.

Note: Many companies do not allow food to be consumed at reception.

Tip: Take your lunch break in a designated break room or break area, or ask a manager to set up a rotating lunch schedule if the reception desk may not be left unattended during lunch. Administrative staff are often happy to share the responsibility of answering the phone for an hour or so to allow the receptionist to take a lunch break.

Note: Some reception desks have a digital receptionist which is an automated function that provides the caller with menu options (such as press 1 to leave a voice message), or alerts the caller that the office is closed for a period of time. A digital receptionist can be set up to switch on and off automatically at certain times, or can be switched on and off by a person when needed.

Always convey a positive attitude

If a caller sounds frustrated, you must remain calm and stay positive. Angry callers are usually not frustrated with the receptionist; they are frustrated about a situation. The receptionist is merely the first person they can tell about it.

Tip: Smile when talking on the phone. A smile creates a friendly tone in your voice.

Dealing with angry customers

If your company provides products or services to customers, you may be on the receiving end of an angry caller. If a caller expresses anger or impatience, do not engage in an argument. Politely convey that you acknowledge the urgency of the call, and transfer the call to the correct person in the company. Do not swear, makes noises such as sighs or grunts, or laugh.

Acknowledge the urgency of the call

No one wants to hear that they are wrong, overreacting or impolite. A caller is usually angry for a reason, and acknowledging their frustration is the first step to a successful engagement with them. You can acknowledge a caller's frustration by saying, "I am sorry about this experience" or "I understand completely".

Transfer the call to the correct person

If someone is available to assist the caller immediately (your company might have a call centre or a product specialist available to assist customers) make sure you transfer the call correctly (see warm and cold transfers). An angry customer will not appreciate being transferred to the wrong department or person. If you do not know who to transfer the call to, place the caller on hold and ask a manager for advice. Remember to tell the manager that the caller has been placed on hold. Always offer the customer the option of having someone call them back or of placing them on hold. Be extra sure that you have their correct contact details if they choose the option of being called back.

Describe the next step

Make sure the customer knows what the next step is. For example, "Ma'am, I am emailing the technical department. They will log a support request and an engineer will contact you as soon as a reference number has been allocated to the query."

Follow up

If you have delivered an important message, follow up and make sure the person for whom the message was intended has received it.

Don't throw anyone under the bus
Never engage in talk that puts down a company employee or department. Remember that you are a member of a team; if you verbally agree with a customer that Joe Jones at your company is always making mistakes, you could end up in trouble. Rather acknowledge the caller's frustration and let them know that you have taken action, for example, that you have escalated their query.

Note: Always follow the company's escalation procedures.

Don't disagree with the customer
Again, no one wants to hear that they are wrong or overreacting. Acknowledge the urgency of the call without engaging with the specific details. There are two reasons for this – one, you might not know how to solve the problem, and two, the customer might feel that they have already explained the entire problem to you and will not want to repeat the details to the person who can actually help them.

Don't cut off a customer in mid-sentence
If you are unable to assist a customer with a query and need to transfer them to another employee or department, wait for an opportunity to let them know that you need to transfer the call. Don't cut them off mid-sentence; it is rude and shows disrespect. Wait for a pause or for a question that allows you a turn to speak. However, if a customer speaks without interruption for a long period of time, politely convey that they have not provided an opportunity to be transferred to the correct department. For example, "Mr Jones, you have reached the reception desk today, may I transfer your call to Mrs Peters in the accounting department?"

Do not make promises that others cannot keep
At times a receptionist might feel obligated to offer a solution to a caller's problem because leaving a caller with no immediate solution or action (such

as successfully directing their call) is not a good feeling. However, promising that an action will take place when you are not absolutely certain that it will, is dangerous business. Imagine telling a customer that Jeff Jones will call them back immediately when Jeff has actually booked a meeting for the entire afternoon. When the customer does not hear from Jeff he or she will think that Jeff has either ignored their call or has not received their message. Neither of these is good for the company's image.

Always convey that you will prioritise the *delivery* of the message. This is different from promising an action on behalf of another person.

Let's look at two scenarios

Scenario 1

An angry caller needs assistance from your IT Department and you need to log a service request with the head engineer.

Receptionist:	Hanna Smith Consultants, good day.
Caller:	My computer is not working again. Since yesterday, after your consultant fixed my email, nothing is working. Nothing! I need someone to fix this right now!
Receptionist:	Certainly. I am logging a service request and marking it as urgent. Who can the engineer contact?
Caller:	Tracy. But I don't want the guy you sent yesterday; send me someone who knows what they are doing.
Receptionist:	Which company are you calling from, Tracy?
Caller:	Epic Designs.
Receptionist:	May I log a direct contact number?
Caller:	They have my number. When are they coming?
Receptionist:	I have sent the service request to the head engineer who will respond as soon as he is available.
Caller:	It better be soon because we can't work.
Receptionist:	I will confirm that he has received this message. Is there anything else they can assist you with today?
Caller:	No, they must just fix the problem.
Receptionist:	Thank you for calling in, Tracy.

- Let's have a closer look at how the receptionist handled this call:

Notice that the caller blurted out the problem without identifying herself. The receptionist acknowledged the urgency of the call then immediately asked who the call should be returned to. In one step the receptionist assured the angry caller that action had begun (the call is receiving attention) and established who was calling.

While the receptionist is logging the service request, the caller makes a remark about the ability of an employee of the company. The receptionist, rather than engaging in a conversation that could put the company employee in a bad light, or anger the caller further by remarking on her comment, proceeds to log the call and adds the caller's name to make it sound more personal. The caller provides the company name when asked.

The receptionist attempts to gather as much information possible in order to provide the engineer with a complete service request. The caller refuses to provide her contact number, and responds with a question, "When are they [an engineer] coming?" The receptionist politely assures the caller that the message is on its way to an important person (the head engineer) without making a promise of a time when an engineer will arrive on site. In this scenario it is important not to make promises for others; the head engineer might not be able to assist the client at the time the receptionist promised.

The caller continues to iterate her frustration during the call. The receptionist, without engaging in an argument or taking sides, provides the caller with a course of action that will be taken, "I have sent the service request to the head engineer who will respond as soon as he is available" and "I will confirm that he has received this message." The receptionist then asks if there is anything else the company can assist her with. This was a nice way to begin to end the call and to check that the engineer would not be surprised by any additional problems at the site. The receptionist thanks the caller for phoning in about the problem.

Additional action: The caller did not provide a contact number, but she did provide the company name she called from. Before sending the service request off to the head engineer the receptionist should look in the company's address book (or client contact list) for the number for Epic Designs and add it to the service request.

Scenario 2

An angry caller does not want to put down the phone until someone helps him.

Receptionist:	Hanna Smith Architects, good morning.
Caller:	I left a message for Joe Jones yesterday. I must come in to sign the quotation so that my crew can start work but he hasn't called me back.
Receptionist:	Mr Jones is not in his office; may I take a message and have him call you back?
Caller:	I just told you he doesn't call back! Find someone who can help me; I have people waiting!
Receptionist:	Who may I ask is calling?
Caller:	Donald Peters. I have left two messages already.
Receptionist:	I apologise for your experience Mr Peters. May I place your call on hold while I find someone who can assist you?
Caller:	Go ahead; I'm holding.

Receptionist places the call on hold and finds someone who can assist the caller.

- Let's have a closer look at how the receptionist handled this call:

The receptionist politely tells the caller that Mr Jones is not in his office and offers to take a message. When it is appropriate, rather tell a client that the person they are looking for is unable to take their call for a reason, such as being in a meeting, conducting a consultation, being out of the office or being on another call. Saying someone is "not available" can sound arrogant – as though they are important and not available to anyone. However, never give out the details of an employee's meetings or calls. It is not acceptable to say who the employee you are taking a message for is talking to or in a meeting with; this is private and confidential company information.

On the other hand, receptionists do not always have access to the agenda of executives, and some executives simply do not wish to disclose their agendas. If you are not able to provide a reason for a staff member not being available to take a call, simply tell the caller that they are not available and offer to take a message or provide the caller the option of being transferred to someone else.

The caller responds angrily when asked if he would like to leave a message for Mr Jones. Rather than starting an argument, the receptionist proceeds to gather the information needed to transfer the call.

The caller provides his name when asked and comments on the numbers of times he has already left a message. The receptionist politely apologises for the experience and asks the client if he is prepared to hold while she finds someone who can assist. The caller agrees.

Note: The daily activities and whereabouts of company employees are confidential. Do not give out details of their activities unless you are certain you are allowed to do so.

You do not need to tolerate offensive language and abuse

If a caller uses inappropriate and offensive language, and engages in a way that is intolerable, you may end the call. Without engaging with the caller (do not scream or swear at the caller) tell them that you are ending the call because you feel that their behaviour is inappropriate and that you would like to ask a manager to assist you. Try to write down as much as you can remember about the call so that the details of the call are properly recorded (unless the call is already being recorded), and inform a supervisor or manager of the incident immediately.

Terms and Definitions

Escalation procedure: The flow of information or queries from one level to another higher level. In many cases a query or issue is escalated to a senior person or specialised department (or external company) in order to resolve an issue that can otherwise not be resolved. Escalations are often limited and allowed only once all other options are exhausted.

IP: Internet Protocol

Mock-up: An example of what a product or service will look like when it is completed. A mock-up is also known as a model or a design; mock-ups are used for demonstration, educational or research purposes.

Soft key: A programmable key on a voice over IP (VoIP) phone. The user can define the function of the physical key.

VoIP: Voice over IP, Internet telephony. Basically, VoIP is the routing of voice communications over the internet.

Chapter four
Business correspondence

Business correspondence is also known as workplace correspondence. In general, workplace correspondence is the writing and exchange of letters, emails, memorandums, proposals, sales documents, and any other communication for the purpose of business. A receptionist is often required to perform communication tasks, even when the company has a communications officer or communications team. Think about it – there is a good chance that every company employee has a company email address. This means that every employee, regardless of their professional title, will exchange a written message with someone at some point. Learning to correspond in a professional manner is important at every level of the company's structure.

Summary of what is included in this section:
- **Business letters**
- **Business emails**
- **Memorandums**
- **Minutes of a meeting**
- **British English vs American English**
- **Changing your proofing language**

Memorandums, letters, meeting minutes and emails are generally written by receptionists, assistants or general administrative staff, whereas sales documents, proposals and marketing materials are generally written by a communications manager or marketing team. However, many companies do not employ full time communications staff and delegate ad hoc communications tasks to their existing employees. A receptionist should therefore be prepared to perform some communications tasks.

Note: This book is written in SASE which, in this case, stands for South African Standard English, not Self Addressed Stamped Envelope. SASE closely resembles the British English model. Some differences between US and British English are noted in this chapter.

Business letters

Before you begin drafting letters and other documents ask for a copy of the company's style guide.

A style guide describes a set of rules for writing and designing company documents. It explains how the company's brand looks and ensures that the company's external documentation (documentation that reaches the outside world) looks consistent. The style guide might include instructions for the appropriate use of the company's logo (including the colour and sizing dos and don'ts), the font to be used, the size and colour of the font, and so on.

Tip: In many cases templates are available for certain documents. Before creating a document from scratch ask if there is a set of templates that you should work from.

Yes, letters still exist, although nowadays most people choose to send emails rather than letters. Emails are sent and delivered within seconds, can be sent to multiple recipients at once, and can be accessed from almost anywhere depending on the email application and device in use. But letters still have a place. In fact, where letters are appropriate, they are often sent as attachments to emails. It is therefore important to know the correct format of a business letter.

Note: Letters are sometimes preferred over emails for certain occasions (such as a letter of condolence), because they convey a particular tone. A letter can also be used for legal reasons.

Tip: If you are attaching a business letter to an email, ensure that the letter follows the conventions of a business letter and that the letter is written on a company letterhead, if applicable.

If you are required to write a letter, the following structure is an example of one way to do it correctly.

The typical layout of a business letter
1. Your company address (also known as the return address) appears at the top right of the document. A return address is not used on a company letterhead as the letterhead usually already contains the details of the return address
2. The date appears below the return address
3. The address of the person to whom the letter is addressed appears at the left of the document, below the date
4. Salutation
5. Subject summary
6. Body text
7. Closing (also known as a valediction or complimentary close)

Your company address
(also known as the
return address).
Date: 15 March 2019

The address of the person
to whom the letter is
addressed.

Dear Mr Jones

Garden Restructuring Proposal for 17 West Avenue
I confirm receipt of your request for a meeting regarding the garden restructuring proposal for 17 West Avenue, Parklands.

I suggest an on-site visit before scheduling a meeting.

Arrangements have been made for access to the property on Mondays and Tuesdays between 08:00 and 13:00.

Yours sincerely,
Jill Evelyn West
Managing Director

Salutations

In formal writing salutations are used to address someone with respect. "Dear" is a formal greeting whereas "Hi" is informal. If you are addressing an employer, company director or head of a department, "Dear" is appropriate; "Hi" should be avoided in formal writing.

Avoid using a person's first name unless the relationship between you and that person is personal (i.e. you know that person very well). Use a surname and title in formal writing. If you do not know the person to whom the letter should be addressed, it is acceptable to write "Dear Sir or Madam" or "To whom it may concern".

Examples of salutations:

Dear Mr Jones

Dear Ms West (Use "Ms" when you are unsure, or do not wish to say, if a woman is married or single)

Dear Dr Jones

Dear Sir or Madam

To whom it may concern

Note: The salutation you have chosen will indicate how you close your letter.

Note: Do not write Dear Mrs Jane Jones. It is Dear Mrs Jones or Dear Jane.

Addressing a group
If you are writing to two people, use both names in the salutation.
Dear Mr Jones and Ms West
Dear Bill and Jane

If you are writing to three or four people, separate names with a comma.
Dear Ms West, Mr Jones, and Mrs Porter
Dear Anne, Jill, Peter, and Dave

If you are writing to more than five people, address the letter to a group.
Dear Sales Department
Dear Colleagues

If you need an informal group salutation that conveys a neutral tone.
Hello Team

Note: In the US the recipient's name is followed by a colon in formal writing, and a comma in informal business writing. The colon is also preferred when writing to a person or group for the first time outside the company. For less formal or personal letters, use a comma.
Dear Colleagues,
Dear Mr. Jones:
Dear Mrs. West and Mr. Peters:
Dear Tom,
Dear Team,

Subject summary
A subject summary is used to tell the addressee what the letter is about. It is not always necessary to include a subject summary, but if you do include one, keep it to a single line. The subject summary can also be written in CAPS (capital letters).

Body text
The body is where you write your letter. The first sentence of your paragraph

should indicate the main idea of the paragraph. For example:

> *We are concerned about the state of the gardens at 17 Doodle Lane.* The rest of the paragraph describes the reasons for concern and includes other information.

Use a new paragraph for each new idea and separate each paragraph with a blank line. For example:

> *We are concerned about the state of the gardens at 17 Doodle Lane. On inspection, the garden had not been watered in over a month, and seedlings had been left in the driveway where visitors park. We also noticed that the main gate to the property was unlocked and unattended.*

> *African Luxury Gardens is inspecting the area around Willows on 12 May 2019. I have asked Mr Jones to assist your team during this time. If you are unable to meet with Mr Jones, please advise my office by no later than 10 April 2019.*

Closing
A formal letter includes a closing, such as:
Yours sincerely,
Yours faithfully,
Yours truly,
Regards,

For example:
Yours sincerely,
Jane Jones
Managing Director

<u>When to use which closing</u>
"Yours sincerely" is used when you have addressed a letter to a named person (e.g. Mr Jones).

"Yours faithfully" is used when you have addressed a letter to "Sir or Madam", "To whom it may concern" or to a department.
"Yours truly" is used when you are somewhat familiar with the addressee.

Note: There are preferred forms of address for particular functions or ranks. For example, if you are writing to an archbishop, the salutation is written as "Your Eminence". If you are required to address officials, ambassadors, generals or high ranking individuals, invest in a resource that is appropriate for your region.

When writing on behalf of someone else
In this example the secretary, Mia Smith, is writing on behalf of the Managing Director, Jill Evelyn West.

Dear Mr Jones
I am concerned about the state of the gardens at 17 Doodle Lane. On inspection, the garden had not been watered in over a month, and seedlings had been left in the driveway where visitors park. We also noticed that the main gate to the property was unlocked and unattended.

African Luxury Gardens is inspecting the area around Willows on 12 March 2019. I have asked Mr Jones to assist your team during this time. If you are unable to meet with Mr Jones, please advise my office by no later than 10 February 2019.

Yours sincerely,
pp *Mia Smith (Signature of Mia Smith)*
Jill Evelyn West

Or

Jill Evelyn West
pp *Mia Smith (Signature of Mia Smith)*

Note: The correct usage of *per procurationem* (pp) is debatable as the term has been taken to mean both "on behalf of" and "through the agency of". It is therefore acceptable to place the "pp" before the name of the person who is not signing. Check with your employer which method they prefer.

Note: pp can also be written as p.p.

Adding a reference

A reference is used to indicate a file number or an account number. If you need to add a reference to a letter, include it after the address or after the date. A reference can be written:

Our ref.: AWC/75H

Your ref.: ACACIA 75, Willows Creek

Insert a date that updates automatically

Templates for letters and other documents sometimes have a date field that updates automatically. If you find this feature useful and would like to add it to your own document templates, use the function in Microsoft Word by selecting **Insert Date and Time** on the **Insert** tab.

Place the cursor at the point where you would like the date to appear and select:

Insert > **Insert Date and Time** > *choose the format of the date or time from the list* > *select* **Update Automatically** > **OK.**

An example of a business letter:

THE INTERIOR DESIGN COMPANY
17 Cruxley Avenue
FULLER BAY
1010

3 February 2019

Mr J Jones
Ground Manager
City Gardens
15 Bigger Avenue
PARK WEST
7171

Our ref.: PARKLANDS/17
Your ref.: BZK/10345

Dear Mr Jones

Concerns identified at inspection of 17 Parklands Lane

I am concerned about the state of the gardens at 17 Parklands Lane. On inspection, the garden had not been watered in over a month, and seedlings had been left in the driveway where visitors park. We also noticed that the main gate to the property was unlocked and unattended.

African Luxury Gardens is inspecting the area around Willows on 20 March 2019. I have asked Mr Peter Jones to assist your team during this time. If you are unable to meet with Mr Jones, please advise my office by no later than 10 February 2019.

I enclose a copy of the inspection report conducted on 15 January 2019.

Yours sincerely,
[Signature]
Jill Evelyn West
Managing Director

Business emails

The address bar

An email is structured in such a way that a return address and business address are not necessary. The address bar of an email contains information that indicates to all parties who the email is to and from, and what the subject of the email is. The company's logo and relevant contact information should appear in the email signature.

The "Cc" (Carbon Copy) field is visible to all recipients. The recipient(s) in the Cc field will receive a copy of the email message.

The "Bcc" (Blind Carbon Copy) field hides the recipient(s) in the Bcc field from the other recipient(s). Use Bcc if you do not want the other recipients to know you have also sent the email to someone else.

The subject line

Use a subject line that is short, makes sense, and accurately describes the content of the email message. If a conversation has been going back and forth, and the subject of the original email has changed, change the subject line or start a new email to discuss the new topic.

Salutations

A business email follows the same salutation conventions as a business letter, but general emails (emails between colleagues) are considered less formal.

Body text

In the business world emails are used for just about anything. It is therefore not surprising that some people receive a few hundred emails a day. It is also no surprise that most people do not read all their emails, or at least do not read all their emails properly.

One topic = one email

Avoid discussing multiple topics in a single email. Most people leave long emails for when they have time to read them, or only focus on the first paragraph of a very long email. If you have written six paragraphs covering six different topics, chances are you will only receive feedback on the first one or two, or a reply much later in the day or even the week, if you receive one at all.

Avoid repeating ideas

Even if you are covering only a single topic, avoid writing pages and pages. Start each paragraph with a single idea and offer information that is new in each consecutive paragraph or sentence.

An email is not a draft of your ideas

Avoid sending emails that are vague and contradictory; only send an email when you know what you want to say.

Avoid immediately responding to emails that caused you to be upset

When you are angry you will say things that you might later regret. Always keep in mind that an email cannot be erased once it has been delivered.

Save complex or important emails as drafts

If you find an email challenging to write, save it to the **Drafts** folder while you are working on it– in most email programs you can simply click on **Save** while you are writing. Do not enter the recipient's email address until you are done in case you accidentally hit **Send** halfway through.

Avoid using exclamation marks and writing in capitals

Exclamation marks and writing in capitals can be considered rude, as though you're shouting at the person. Exclamation marks and capitals can also take emphasis away from important comments that appear elsewhere in the text.

Ask yourself, should I rather pick up the phone?
Email is not the correct medium for every kind of conversation. If you find that the content of an email is complex, and the meaning of the text does not convey your thoughts clearly, consider giving the person a call.

Keep private conversations out of the workplace
Avoid sending private messages that could be hurtful or offensive, or which disclose confidential information about other employees.

Attachments
If you are sending an email with an attachment, always check that the correct file is attached before sending the email. The easiest way to check an attachment is to open it.
Ensure you appropriately name documents that will be attached to emails. A document named 72364876478dfg.pdf is confusing, especially when the email contains numerous attachments that should be viewed in a particular order.
P Jones Financial Statement 2019.pdf looks a lot better than a string of numbers.

Note: Some documents follow a specific naming convention to include the date and time the document was scanned or created (or other information the company requires).

Tip: If you are scanning a document, check that the document displays correctly before attaching it to an email; it is frustrating to receive a document that is upside down.

Emoticons
Avoid using emoticons when composing a business email. Emoticons should only be used between friends and colleagues who are well acquainted.

Closing an email

An email usually includes a formal company signature. If the signature includes a standard closing do not repeat that, but if the signature does not include a closing, the following options are suitable for ending standard business emails:

Kind regards,
Best regards,
Regards,
Sincerely,

If you would like to convey a friendlier or more personal tone, use:
Warm regards,

For example:
Warm regards,
Jill Evelyn West
Managing Director
Hanna Smith Consultants

A note about email signatures:

Most companies use email signatures as a rule. If you do not have a signature, ask the IT Department to add one to your emails. Signatures look professional and save time.

Reply and Reply All

When you reply to a message for the first time, include a greeting such as "Hi" ("Hi" is used when you know the recipient; use "Dear" for a formal greeting). However, consecutive conversations should not include a greeting at every turn. Think of it like a verbal conversation between two people – you do not say "Hi" every time it is your turn to speak.

Use "Reply All" with caution

If you receive an email from a colleague, and that colleague has copied in other recipients (such as an entire department) be respectful of the group when replying to everyone. If you are sending a personal message back to the sender (like "Cool Beans!"), check that you are not sending it to everyone who was copied in. Only use Reply All when you have something valuable to say to the entire group.

Tip: Never use **Reply All** to send a personal message. It is frustrating for the group to receive replies on messages that have nothing to do with the original message.

Check the email thread

If you are forwarding an email thread (an entire email conversation) to someone who was not included in the original recipient list, check the thread for information that is confidential or that might not be appropriate to send to them. If the thread contains such information, consider writing a new email that contains only the information that is relevant.

Memorandums

A memorandum (or memo) is a form of internal communication between company employees. Memos are used to inform staff of events, policy changes, changes to meeting procedures, office etiquette, rules for using the internet or social media, or any other communication intended to convey a general message to staff.

An example of a memorandum:

Company Logo

MEMORANDUM

To: All administrative staff
From: M Rothmann
        Marketing and Communications Manager
Date: 17 November 2019

BUSINESS WRITING SKILLS TRAINING

A course on business writing will soon be held for the admin staff. The course will be presented by Ms J Jones from The Hanna Smith Agency.

DATE: 4 December 2019
VENUE: Room 7
TIME: 08:15 – 15:00

Registration forms are available at the reception desk for those who wish to attend. Please return the completed form to Alice by end of business on 25 November 2019.
Refreshments and a light lunch will be provided on the veranda at 11:30. If you have any special meal requests please indicate your preference on the registration form.

[Signature]
M Rothmann
Marketing and Communications Manager

This is a basic example of a memo. Memos can consist of a few sentences or be as long as a few pages. Your company might have a template on which memos are drafted, so always remember to ask if a template is available. If not, the example given here is sufficient. You might even like to create your own template when you are familiar with the company's tone of voice.

Note: A company's **tone of voice** is their personality. It is both what they say and how they say it. A company's tone of voice can be professional, quirky, laid back, or sophisticated. Compare working at a law firm to working at an animation studio; the internal and external communications of these companies will both look and sound very different. It is up to you to discover the tone of voice of your company and to apply it to the daily communicative tasks that have been assigned to you. If you are unsure if a certain communication is acceptable or not, ask before sending it out.

Example of tone of voice:
Imagine you are working for an animation studio and your company is hip and quirky.
Your out of office reply might look like this:
Oops! I am travelling.
If you need to ask someone a question immediately, hit them at info@mystudioexample.com (this is a fictitious email address).
If you can wait until the credits have rolled, I will respond in September.

If you are working at a law firm your out of office reply will look something like this:
I am out of the office until 7 June 2019 and unable to respond to your query.
For urgent enquiries, contact admin@hnmpattorneys.com (this is a fictitious email address).
If you have not received a reply to your query within 24 hours, please contact our office directly.

Minutes of a meeting

The minutes of a meeting is an official record of a specific meeting.
As a receptionist it is not likely that you will be asked to take the minutes of a meeting; assistants and executive assistants are often given this task as they are familiar with the industry terminology and have some knowledge of

what the meeting is about. Meetings can also sometimes run for a few hours or take place at a venue outside of the office or even after standard business hours. Unless absolutely necessary, a company will not leave the reception desk unattended for hours at a time, or require a receptionist to work at an external location. However, companies which have a smaller workforce might require the receptionist to take the minutes of a meeting, or to stand in for a secretary or assistant who is on leave.

The chair and the secretary
The chairperson or chair ensures that the meeting runs smoothly and that it follows the points on the agenda. The chair also ensures that all the attendees are equally represented. If a vote needs to be taken, the chair ensures that the voting process is fair and accurate.

The secretary is responsible for arranging the meeting, and that includes ensuring that documentation, stationery, accommodation, technical requirements, catering, and seating are arranged. If a meeting takes place in an office, the secretary confirms that the venue is available and clean. This person also checks that the chair does not miss a point on the agenda. The secretary takes the minutes of the meeting.

The procedure for a meeting
1. Send a notice of the meeting to all who are required to attend
2. Send an agenda and any documentation that needs to be reviewed in preparation for the meeting
3. Set up an attendance register and the minutes of the last meeting (if applicable)
4. Make a summary of what was said and decided in the meeting
5. Prepare the minutes of the meeting
6. The chairperson signs off the minutes as correct

1. Notice of a meeting

Send a meeting notice to all the parties who are required to attend.

The notice must include a short summary of the purpose of the meeting, time, date and venue.

Note: Ensure that a company email signature is displayed if a notice is sent via email.

Example of a meeting notice:

NOTICE OF MEETING (in the email subject line)

To: Marketing Department

YEARLY SPONSORSHIP REVIEW

The annual sponsorship review will take place on Friday, 3 August 2019 in Room 123 at 13:00.

If anyone would like to include suggestions for the agenda, please submit these in writing by end of business 15 July 2019.

Kind regards

M Harraway (Include the name, title and position if it is not displayed in a signature)

Executive Assistant to Mr Jones

Note: If the notice is sent via courier, include a telephone number or email address for RSVP purposes.

2. Agenda and documentation

Consolidate an agenda for the meeting from the list of points you have been given by the secretary and the attendees. If an attendee added a point to be discussed that is not applicable to the meeting, the secretary will remove it from the list before the final agenda is sent.

Attach the agenda and relevant documentation in an email or in an envelope if it's being sent by courier. If you are sending documents via a courier service, ensure there is enough time for the parcel to reach the addressee. Always use a reliable and secure document courier when sending sensitive company documents.

Example of an agenda:

Annual Sponsorship Review
Meeting Agenda
3 August 2019
Room 123

1. Welcome (required if an opening statement is made)
2. Attendance (or Present)
3. Apologies
4. Minutes of the previous meeting
5. Annual Sponsorship Review
    i. Sponsorships in place for 2020
    ii. Sponsorships pending
        a. Company A
        b. Company B
        c. Issues with Company B
    iii. Strategies to maximise efficiency of sponsor funds
        a. Strategy 1
        b. Strategy 2
        c. Strategy 3
    iv. New sponsors for 2021
6. Remarks
7. Date of next meeting
8. Adjournment (or Closing)

Tip: Once you have received all the RSVPs make a list of the attendees and create a column called "Sent" next to their name. As the document courier picks up the parcel, or an email is sent, make a note in the column.

Name	Sent	Delivery method
Mrs P Jones	Yes	Email
Mr K Smith	Yes	Email
Miss L Lee	Yes	DC Couriers

3. Set up an attendance register and the minutes of the last meeting (if applicable)

Ensure that you have an attendance register ready for everyone to sign. Present the minutes of the last meeting to the secretary before the meeting is called to order. The secretary will ensure the minutes of the previous meeting are signed by the chair.

Example of an attendance register:

Annual Sponsorship Review
Attendance Register
3 August 2019
Room 123

Ms Jane Jones	[Signature]
Dr Peter Smith	[Signature]
Prof. Kelly Wagner	[Signature]
Mr Peter Burns	[Signature]

4. Take notes of decisions and persons responsible for actions

- Do not try to write down everything that everyone says

Listen attentively and make a clear note of any decisions that are taken and the persons responsible for completing various tasks.

Tip: Number the pages you are writing on in case they fall or are jumbled.

- Use abbreviations to write long or complicated words

Prepare an abbreviation for each attendee's name beforehand so that you do not need to write out their name every time you wish to note what they have said. This is especially useful when two or more attendees have the same first name or surname.

Prepare separate sheets of paper with headings for each topic of discussion from the agenda.

5. Prepare the minutes of the meeting

Write these briefly and accurately, and as soon as possible after the meeting; prepare the minutes while the meeting is fresh in your memory. Minutes are written in the past tense – for example, Mr J Jones said, not Mr J Jones says.

Example of meeting minutes:

Minutes of the annual sponsorship meeting
3 August 2019

PRESENT

Mr J Jones (Chairperson), Mr P Smith (Secretary), Mr L Lee, Mrs SP White, Miss A Deale

1. Welcome

    Mr J Jones welcomed the attendees.

2. Apologies for absence
   Prof. K Kelly, Miss P Smith

3. Minutes of the previous meeting
   The minutes of the last meeting were accepted as correct.

4. New sponsorships
   Miss Deale pointed out that at least two new sponsorships are required to secure the venue at Gala Estate. Mrs White proposed waiting for confirmation from both new and existing sponsors before sending out invitations. Mr Lee will seek confirmation from all sponsors by 1 September 2019.

5. Existing sponsorships
   Mr Lee stated that Big Sky Gardening will not be sponsoring any events in 2020.

6. Arrangements for the annual luncheon
   Mrs White proposed a smaller venue than usual for the secretaries' annual luncheon. Mr Deale agreed that, based on the cost of securing venues such as Gala Estates for bigger events, the staff events should be held at less expensive venues. Mrs White will secure a new venue for the secretaries' luncheon in 2020 by 1 November.

7. Date of next meeting
   The next meeting will be held on 2 December 2019 at 13:00.

8. Closing
   The meeting closed at 17:55.

_____
Mr J Jones   Date: _____
Chairperson

Terms used in formal meetings

Addendum:	An additional document
Adjourn:	The meeting is postponed to a later date
Advisory:	A person or company which provides advice, but does not influence the decision
Amendment:	A change to a motion that does not alter the original meaning of the motion
Agenda:	A list of items to be discussed at a meeting
Casting vote:	A vote that decides the outcome. The casting vote is usually an extra vote given to the chairperson
Held over:	The matter will be dealt with in a future meeting
Motion:	A motion is proposed (or introduced for consideration) so that a decision can be made. A motion, if accepted, becomes a resolution
Point of order:	A formal way of pointing out that a procedure is not being followed, or a rule is being broken. The chair will rule on whether the complaint is justified or not
Quorum:	A minimum number of people needed to conduct business in a meeting
Resolution:	A motion that has been accepted is a resolution
Treasurer:	The person responsible for the finances
Unanimous:	A unanimous decision is a decision where everyone agreed (all in favour)

Use templates and save time

If you have not been given a set of company templates to work from, use professional templates available in your application. In Microsoft Office®, applications such as Word, Excel, PowerPoint® and Publisher® provide countless templates to choose from. To open and edit a template, select the **File** tab in your application, select **New,** and choose a template from the list or search for templates online.

One grammar rule I must explain

The New Receptionist is not a book about effective writing or grammar.

However, there is one grammar rule that often gets the best of us, and I am including it here because it is by far one of the most common writing mistakes people make.

A versus an
A before consonants, *an* before vowels, right? Sort of.
The rule actually is: *A* before words that **start with a consonant sound**, *an* before words that **start with a vowel sound**.
As a reminder, vowels are the letters a, e, i, o, and u.

For example:
A unique look (unique sounds like it starts with "y")
I will be there in under an hour (hour sounds like it starts with "o")
A cat
An invitation
A unanimous decision (unanimous sounds like it starts with "y")
An undisputed decision

Note: If you need an English grammar book, I highly recommend *The Blue Book of Grammar and Punctuation* by Jane Straus.

British English vs American English
In the introduction of this book I spoke about how the internet has created a connected global community. One of the consequences of the ease of communicating globally is that we adopt each other's habits, and language is a good example of this. In South Africa we follow the British English model, but this does not mean that you will not encounter American English in South Africa or other parts of the world in the professional workplace.
This section highlights some of the most common differences between British and American English.

Punctuation in titles
American English favours the use of a full-stop after the abbreviation of a title such as Dr. or Ms. whereas British English does not. (Dr is an

abbreviation for the title Doctor.)

However, in British English full stops are used when the last letter of the title does not end with the same letter as the abbreviation.

Doctor = **Dr**

Professor = Prof.

Writing addresses

A British formal letter places the return address and date at the top right (look at the examples provided earlier in this chapter), whereas the American business letter format prefers to place the return address and date at the left of the page.

Closings

American English and British English use different closings in formal letters, for example:

American English	American English
Yours truly,	Yours faithfully,
Sincerely yours,	Yours sincerely,

Note: "Faithfully yours", while not incorrect, is rarely used. In British English "Yours truly" is used in informal writing.

Other differences between American English and British English
"Ou" vs "o" in spelling

American English	British English
Color	Colour
Behavior	Behaviour
Humor	Humour
Neighbor	Neighbour

"Er" vs "re" in spelling

American English	British English
Center	Centre
Meter	Metre

"Ize" vs "ise" in spelling

American English	British English
Apologize	Apologise
Recognize	Recognise
Organize	Organise

Note: In British English, the "ize" spelling is also accepted. There are, however, a few words that must be spelled "ise" in both American and British English. These include words like exercise and supervise.

Words that differ

American English	British English
Vacation	Holiday
Apartment	Flat
Check	Bill
French fries	Chips
Trailer	Caravan
Swimsuit	Costume
Comforter	Duvet
Soccer	Football
Elevator	Lift

Date format

American English	British English
mm/dd/yyyy	dd/mm/yyyy
May 22, 2019	22 May 2019

Consistency is key

There are many examples of differences between American English and British English. If this topic interests you, enrol in an advanced English learning course that offers this topic as a subject on its own. In a professional office, consistency is key. Choose to follow either the American or British model in one document or set of documents.

Tip: Set your proofing language to check if your writing is consistent.

Changing your proofing language

If you are checking a document for errors, ensure that the correct proofing language is selected.

- In Word, select **Review > Language > Set Proofing Language.**
- In Outlook, select **New Email** on the Mail view to create a new email, then select **Review > Language > Set Proofing Language.**
- Select a language from the list.
- Check that **Do not check spelling or grammar** is cleared.

Terms and Definitions

Ad hoc: A task that is done when the need arises, not as part of a routine.

End of business: The end of the work day, usually 16:30 or 17:00. End of business is also called close of business.

External documentation: Documentation that will find its way to the outside world, such as to clients, the general public, vendors and business partners. Examples include proposals, advertisements, user manuals and general communications.

Internal documentation: Documentation that is for use inside the company and by the company employees. This can include company policies (such as dress codes or social media policies), employee manuals, training manuals (many companies require employees to familiarise themselves with the internal software the company uses such as CRM software), stock lists, client lists, memorandums, leave forms, documents relating to key internal processes, and much more.

I.e. versus e.g.: I.e. is used to say "that is", whereas e.g. is used to say "for example".

Letterhead: A document template that contains the address, postal address, contact information, VAT number, company registration number, logo, and any other company information. The letterhead information usually appears at the top of the page in the document header, but can also appear at the side, or extend to the footer section of the document. A header and footer can be set to appear on all the pages of the document, on odd or even pages, or only on the first page.

p.p.: *per procurationem*. This indicates that a letter is signed on behalf of someone else.

Salutation: A salutation is a greeting such as "Dear".

Valediction: A closing such as "Yours sincerely".

Chapter five
Terms you will come across in a business environment

Terms used in a business environment will include both universal and industry related expressions. Universal terms are general expressions that you will find used in any industry, such as "AGM" and "Account", whereas industry related terms are those that are specific to a particular industry. For example, an actor or voice-over artist applies for a job by going to an *audition*, whereas an accountant applies for a job by going to an *interview*. *Audition* is therefore regarded as an industry related term because it describes an event that occurs in the entertainment industry.

Summary of what is included in this section:
· **Terms used in business**

Familiarise yourself with the terms in this section to build confidence before entering the business world. If you come across an industry related term or acronym that is not included in this list, make a note of it and look it up in a reputable dictionary.

Note: Industry *jargon* is the vocabulary of a particular industry. Jargon is also called *lingo.*

Note: Acronyms are words formed from the first letters of other, usually longer words. Acronyms are pronounced as words. For example, radar is an acronym for "radio detection and ranging". Similarly, UNESCO is an acronym for the United Nations Educational, Scientific and Cultural Organization.

Terms used in business

Many of the terms listed in this section have more than one meaning. The definitions of these terms are limited to how they might be used in a business environment.

Account: A client's business. Account managers are tasked with retaining and managing accounts. Key accounts are specific or important accounts, and a key account manager is often responsible for the accounts of a particular client or group of clients.

Agent: An individual or company that provides services on behalf of another company. An agent can also be a representative of a company, such as a sales agent.

AGM (Annual General Meeting): A meeting that is held once a year. The purpose of an AGM is to report on the company's activities and finances for the year, and to plan for the year ahead.

Asset: The elements of a business that are owned. Assets are described as tangible (physical) assets and intangible (non-physical) assets. Tangible assets include cars, buildings, and machinery, whereas intangible assets include business accounts, skills, and trademarks. Assets have an economic value.

Acquisition: The process of attaining something. An acquisitions manager is someone who looks for and closes deals. An acquisition also occurs when one company purchases another company.

B2B (business to business): B2B is used to describe transactions such as sales and services between businesses. When a business sells products or services to a consumer, it is called B2C (business to consumer).

Benchmark: A standard against which something can be tested. Benchmarking is used to evaluate and compare certain aspects of a company with those of another competitor company, or internally within the same company.

Brand: An image, text, or combination by which a company or individual is recognised. Microsoft, Coca-Cola, Amazon and Samsung are examples of brands.

Business plan: A well-documented plan to accomplish a specific goal. Some reasons for writing a business plan include obtaining an investment or a bank loan for your business.

Capital: The word capital may be used to refer to the money used to start a business as well as further investment by the owner in the business. Capital is also used when total liabilities are deducted from total assets illustrating the net worth of a business.

Commission: An amount of money (usually calculated as a percentage) paid to an employee or agent for the successful sale of goods or services.

Competitor: An individual or business that sells to and competes in the same market as you. Apple and Samsung are competitors in the mobile phone market.

Contract: An agreement that is binding; a contract is enforceable by law. Documents that supplement contracts are called appendices and annexures. Michalsons Attorneys (2016) defines an annexure as "a separate document from the agreement [such as a] report" and an appendix as "[a] part of the agreement ... that is invariably critical to the validity of the agreement".

Copy: Copy is another name for the words on a page such as the text in a magazine article. Copy is usually written by a copywriter. In advertising, copy is the text used in an advertisement.

Corporations: Very large firms that are run by shareholders. A corporate environment, on the other hand, is any professional business environment that incorporates policies and a culture typically found in much larger companies.

Corporate culture: The way a company interacts with its employees, clients and other businesses. It is who they are and how they choose to work. This includes the way they dress, the hours they choose to work, their management style, how they view learning and extra-curricular achievements, and how they engage with their clients and business partners. Corporate culture covers the values and beliefs of a company.

CRM (Customer Relationship Manager): The person who is responsible for retaining a customer's business or acquiring new business accounts. A CRM is also known as an account manager.

CRM software: Software relating to customer management. CRM software helps businesses manage client data, contacts, marketing, contracts, lead generation and lead management, and reports.

Development: In the IT industry development refers to the programming of computer software. A development team is a team of software engineers. A developer is also known as a programmer.

Dividends: Profits that are paid to the shareholders of a company. Dividends are usually paid once per year.

Entrepreneur: An individual who starts their own business. Entrepreneurs are creative thinkers who start new businesses in order to meet a specific need in a market. Elon Musk and Steve Jobs are famous entrepreneurs.

ERP (Enterprise Resource Planning) system: At its most basic, ERP is a system that combines and simplifies many different processes into one unified process. An ERP system is a software system that assists with a business's internal processes. Microsoft Dynamics® 365 is an enterprise resource planning and customer relationship management application.

Expenses: Costs incurred by a business during its trading to generate revenue. Costs that a company carries in order to conduct business can include electricity, rent, petrol, stationery, and salaries. Expenses are also called disbursements.

Forex: Foreign exchange. When currency from one country is exchanged (sold) for currency of another country.

Fortune 500 company: Published by *Fortune* magazine, The Fortune 500 is a list published annually ranking the 500 most successful (by total revenue) publicly and privately held corporations in the United States. The Fortune 100, The Fortune 1000, Global 500, and 100 Best Companies to Work For, are other lists also published by *Fortune*.

Gross: Gross profit is the surplus that remains after the cost of sales (cost of producing the product or service) has been deducted from the generated revenue.

HR (Human Resources): The Human Resources Department provides support to the staff. HR manages the payroll, benefits, disciplinary actions, dismissals and hiring of new employees; this department is also responsible for ensuring the company abides by certain laws and regulations.

Independent contractor: An individual or company that provides goods and services to another company. Independent contractors are not employees of the company which makes use of their goods or services.

Inventory: The goods or materials in stock (at hand). Stock can be held in a small stockroom or in a large warehouse depending on the size of the company.

IPO (Initial Public Offering): The process of selling shares in a private corporation to investors for the first time.

KPI (Key Performance Indicator): A measurement that is used to track a company's performance. KPIs are used to track the progress of a wide range of business activities, and indicate how far each activity is from reaching its goal. The KPIs that can be measured for a sales department, for example, include: number of leads, number of leads converted to monthly sales, weekly sales, annual sales, outstanding sales for the month, and so on.

KPO (Key Performance Objective): This benchmark determines how well an employee or team is performing against a set goal. Goals that can be set for employees include monetary targets, number of clients visited monthly or quarterly, response times to queries, project completion rate, and so on.

Liabilities: A liability is something that is owed, for example money owed to the bank or outside contractors. Liabilities are therefore debts (owed by the business) that arise during the normal course of business.

Liquidation: Liquidation is the process of selling a business's assets in order to pay creditors. Liquidation brings all business operations to an end and the business closes its doors when the process is complete. Liquidation usually occurs when a company can no longer pay its debts.

Logistics: The management of movement of goods and services (either physical goods or the organization of the process of moving services) from the company to the consumer.

Market: The individuals and organisations who are available to buy a company's products or services. In other words, it's the people or companies who have a need for your product or service.

Market share: The total number of customers who are actually buying your product compared to those who are buying from a competitor (usually calculated as a percentage). A customer can be a person or a company.

Marketing: The promotion (advertising) of a company's goods and services.

Merger: When two companies join as one more efficient or stronger company.

NDA (non-disclosure agreement): An agreement between parties to not disclose certain information to any other party. A non-disclosure agreement is beneficial when confidential information needs to be disclosed to potential business partners or investors. A non-disclosure agreement is also called a confidentiality agreement.

Net: Net profit is the profit after all expenses have been deducted. Simply put, it is the money the company actually makes. Net profit is also called the bottom line.

Networking: Using existing contacts (people you know) to meet other new contacts for the purpose of doing business with them in some way.

Outsource: Companies outsource certain functions to other companies or individuals so that they do not need to hire employees to perform the function internally e.g. hiring cleaning services or security services. Outsourcing saves costs and is useful when a service is needed for a short period of time.

Performance review: An assessment of an employee's work duties. A performance review (also known as a performance appraisal) is usually conducted once or twice a year by a manager. Employees' KPOs are assessed in a performance review.

Portfolio: A business portfolio is a list of the business's assets. Assets can include investments, property, products, other businesses, and brands.

Preliminary: Preliminary means "to do in preparation" or "to do before". For example, a preliminary meeting is a meeting that is held to discuss challenges and opportunities before final decisions are made.

Profit: The amount of money a company makes after all the expenses have been subtracted.

Proxy: A proxy is someone who acts on behalf of another person; a proxy is also called an agent. For example, a proxy may be appointed to vote on behalf of an absent member at an annual committee meeting.

R&D (Research and Development): Research departments are usually tasked with finding new ways of doing things or coming up with new products the company can sell.

Retrenchment: The process of reducing staff due to operational changes or when the company has suffered losses. Retrenching staff can assist a company to stabilize its financial position.

Revenue: Revenue is the total income made before expenses are subtracted. Revenue is generated from the day-to-day running of the business. Revenue is also known as turnover, and is typically calculated annually.

RFT (Request for Tender): A formal invitation to bid on the supply of specific goods or services.

ROI (Return on Investment): The size of profits or losses in relation to an amount invested. It is what investors look at when deciding whether they should invest in a project.

Shareholder: An individual or a company who owns shares of stock in a corporation. A shareholder is also called a stockholder.

SME: Small to medium-sized enterprise. An SME is somewhere between a very small company and a large enterprise. The European Commission defines an SME as an enterprise that is small if the company headcount is less than 50, and medium-sized if the company headcount is less than 250. In South Africa, a business is small if the company headcount is less than 50, and medium-sized if the company headcount is less than 200 (100 in the Agricultural sector). Turnover is also used to define whether a company is an SME. Companies defined as SMEs will differ from country to country..

SMME: Small, medium and micro-sized enterprise.

Supply chain: The total management of the process of delivering goods from the raw creation phase to the finished product that goes to a consumer. That is, the process of taking a raw material, making a product, and delivering that product to a customer.

SWOT analysis (Strengths, Weakness, Opportunities, and Threats): A planning tool that companies use to analyse a product or a service. A SWOT analysis is usually performed before a new product or service is developed and released to the market. The product's strengths and weaknesses (mainly internal concerns) are evaluated, and opportunities and threats (usually external factors that can influence the product's success) that could emerge from the product's release are analysed.

Tender: Government departments, private organisations and businesses make publicly known that they require certain goods or services (see RFT). A tenderer then makes an offer to do the work and estimates the cost. A tender must usually be submitted within a set of guidelines.

Trademark: A trademark is an image (logo) or a word mark (text) that identifies and protects a brand or a product.
MyBrand™ – Unregistered trademark.
MyBrand® – Registered trademark. A trademark is registered with a trademark office in one or more countries. Adobe® is a trademark of Adobe in the United States and/or other countries.

Work for Hire agreement: An agreement between a company and an independent contractor. Work for hire work is usually commissioned; it is particularly common in the entertainment industry.

Vendor: An individual or a company that sells a service or a product. Vendors can be contracted to sell services or products on behalf of companies.

VMR (Virtual Meeting Room): An online meeting room. In virtual meetings, participants share video, audio, and files on a dedicated internet space. Companies typically purchase VRM software and video conferencing packages for reliability and security.

Chapter six
The company structure

Most companies are structured a certain way to ensure a particular level of compliance with world trends. An organizational or company structure also ensures a shared understanding of what is expected from certain positions within the company. The role players within a company are given specific titles, and these can be confusing to someone who is just entering the business world.

Take note of the corporate titles and roles in this section to build confidence when dealing with executive and non-executive staff.

Note: Corporate titles, and roles associated with corporate titles, can differ from company to company.

Summary of what is included in this section:
· **Corporate titles and roles you might come across in a business environment**

Corporate titles and the roles they fulfil
Shareholders

The shareholders (also known as stockholders) of a company own shares in the company, and are its owners. Shareholders can be individuals or companies. The shareholders are not involved with the daily operations of the company.

Board of Directors

Together with the chief executive officer (CEO) and the chief financial officer (CFO), the board of directors is responsible for running the company. The board of directors report to the shareholders.

Chair (also chairperson, chairman, or chairwoman)

The board of directors votes for the chair, and the person selected is then head of the board of directors. The chair sometimes provides support to the CEO or president, although this is not always the case.

Chief Executive Officer (CEO)

The chief executive officer (CEO) reports to the board of directors; he or she is responsible for the company's strategy. In British English the CEO is also called the managing director (MD).

The CEO can also be called the president of the company.

Note: The corporate titles that define specific roles within a company may differ depending on the company's geographical location.

Chief Financial Officer (CFO)

The chief financial officer reports to the chief executive officer. The CFO is responsible for the company's finances, including financial planning and risk planning.

Chief Operations Officer (COO)

The chief operations officer reports to the chief executive officer. The COO is responsible for the daily operation of the company.

Chief Technical Officer (CTO)

The chief technical officer reports to the chief executive officer. The CTO is responsible for the technological aspects of a company.

Note: The CEO, CFO, COO and CTO form the most senior level of management within a company (also known as top management).

Director

A company can have many directors; they typically oversee particular areas of the company. For example, the human resources director oversees the activities of the Human Resources Department.

Supervisor and manager

A supervisor is often referred to as a first-line (or first level) manager. Supervisors work directly with the employees (or non-management staff).

Note: Middle managers report to senior managers. A middle manager can be a sales manager, communications manager, or a marketing manager. Supervisors typically report to middle management.

Employees

Employees are often skilled individuals who work at a non-executive level.

Chapter seven

General computer skills for the receptionist

In today's world you need to know your way around a computer. Receptionists are expected to know the basics of a word processing application like Word, how to send and receive emails, and how to save and print documents to various formats. This section provides an overview of overlooked or underused functions in Word, and offers help for working with PDFs, proofing tools, calendars, images, and other general functions.

Summary of what is included in this section:
· **Working with document formats**
· **Editing a PDF document**
· **Working with styles in Microsoft Word**
· **Proofing tools**
· **Microsoft Outlook®**
· **Outlook Tasks and Reminders**
· **Making images smaller**
· **Sending marketing and other copy to a professional printer**
· **General IT security tips**

Note: If you need *from-scratch* training on a specific application, ask your instructor if learning material is available on the company's website or portal. Many companies offer free training to their employees. If you need computer training and nothing is available to you via your company's learning channels, invest in learning material from your nearest bookstore or purchase a book online.

Unless otherwise indicated, all the examples in this section refer to either Microsoft Office 2016, Office 2019 or Office 365. These are currently the versions of Office most companies will have a licence for. If you are using an earlier version of Office or a different word processing application like Corel® WordPerfect® or Apple® Pages®, refer to the relevant help available for your product.

Note: Office 365 is a cloud-based subscription model for home and business users. This means that instead of purchasing a productivity suite like Office 2019 outright and installing it on-site on one computer, a home or business user pays a monthly or yearly subscription for the Office 365 suite and downloads or accesses the applications from the internet. The advantage of Office 365 is that it has more features than the on-premises solution, and is always up to date.

This section refers to the Microsoft Office ribbon, tabs, and dialog box launcher. Familiarise yourself with their location so that you are able to follow the examples. If you are using Office 365 or Office for Mac, the ribbon icons will have a slightly different look to those in figure 1.

Figure 1

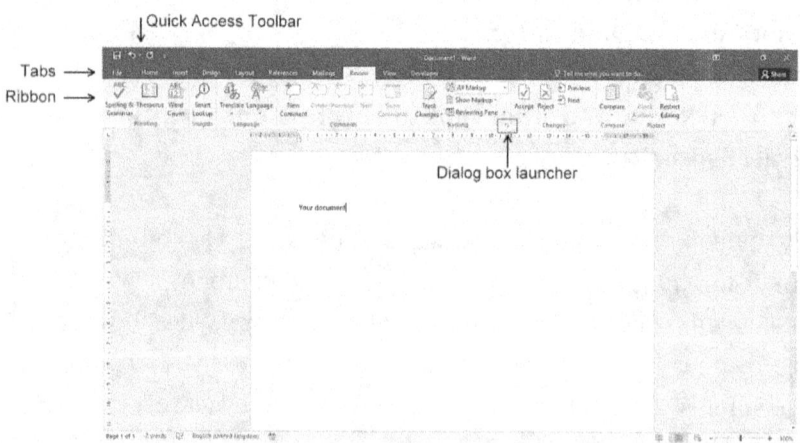

Working with document formats
Saving documents as PDF (Portable Document Format) files
PDF files are widely used for their compatibility with a wide range of

programs. As the name suggests, PDF files are portable (they can easily be exchanged between users and applications) and compact.

Note: Originally created by Adobe in the early 1990s, PDF is an open standard maintained by the International Organization for Standardization (ISO). Read more about the history of PDF at
https://acrobat.adobe.com/za/en/acrobat/about-adobe-pdf.html.

PDF files have come a long way since the 1990s; today they are editable and can contain text, images, videos, links, and audio files. The advantage of saving and sending a file as a PDF is that you know exactly what the file will look like to the receiver, which is not always the case with other file formats. A PDF file looks exactly the same to any user who opens it because the view is not dependent on the application that was originally used to create it or the operating system the user is using. This is good news when you are sending files to clients and executives.

Adobe® Acrobat® Pro DC is a professional choice for companies that work with PDF documents. Acrobat Pro DC has all the tools you need to create and edit PDF files, including exporting PDFs to Word, rearranging pages, enhancing scanned documents, adding comments, and electronically signing documents. However, reliable and secure PDF editing software is not free, and might not be installed on computers where the users are not required to edit PDF files. If you do not have a software program like Acrobat Pro DC, you should at least have a PDF viewer to open and view PDF files. If you cannot view a PDF file, ask your IT Department to install a PDF viewer on your computer.

Almost every word processing application will allow you to save or export a document as a PDF file. Make sure you are familiar with the location of the option in the program you are using.

- Option 1

In Word, the **Save As** dialog box provides many options in the **Save as type** dropdown list. Choose PDF (*.pdf) (or similar description depending on the version of Word you are using) to save a document as a PDF.

In Word, select **File** > **Save As** > *Browse to location* > *Enter file name in* **File name** *field* > *Choose* **PDF** (*.pdf) *from* **Save as type** *dropdown list* > **Save.**

- Option 2

In Word, select: **File** > **Print** > *Select* **Microsoft Print to PDF** *from the Printer options list* > **Print** > *Browse to location* > *Enter file name in* **File name** *field* > ***Choose* PDF Document** (*.pdf) *from the* **Save as type** *dropdown list* > **Save.**

Note: PDF can be written as PDF or pdf.

Note: I need help! Every application should have a **Help** function. Later versions of Office, for example, have a ***Tell me what you want to do...*** field (or press Alt+Q) on the ribbon. As you type your question in the field, available help topics will populate the dropdown list. Select the description that fits your query and view the associated help document, or jump to perform the action described in the list.

Try it out:

In Word:

In the *Tell me what you want to do* field, begin to type, "Save as PDF".

The list that appears looks something like this:

Save

Save As

Save As Other Format

Explore Quick Parts

Get Help on "Save As PDF"

Smart Lookup on "Save as PDF"

If you select: **Save As Other Format** > **PDF XPS**, the dialog box where you perform the action of saving the document as a PDF will open.

If you select *Get Help on Save as PDF*, a dialog box with help topics will open.

Editing a PDF document

If you are required to edit the content of a PDF file, either edit the file in a PDF document editor, or convert the document to a Word document (.doc or .docx) to edit the file in Word.

- Option 1

In Acrobat Pro DC, open the PDF document: **File** > **Open** > *Browse to the file location* > *Select the file and choose* **Open.** When the file is open, select: **Edit** > **Edit Text & Images** (or Edit PDF on the right hand pane).
You are now able to edit the text and the images of the PDF document.

- Option 2

In Acrobat Pro DC, open the PDF document: **File** > **Open** > *Browse to the file location* > *Select the file and choose* **Open.** When the file is open, select: **File** > **Export To** > **Microsoft Word** > **Word Document** > *Browse to the location* > **Save.**
The document will export.

If the text of the new document appears as images that are not editable, use the **Recognise Text** tool in Acrobat Pro DC before exporting the document to Word.
In Acrobat Pro DC, open the PDF document: **File** > **Open** > *Browse to the file location* > *Select the file and choose* **Open.**
On the right hand pane, select: **Enhance Scans** > *Choose* **Recognize Text** *from the* **Enhance Scans** *toolbar* > *choose* **In This File** *from the dropdown list* > *choose the* **Recognize Text** *command.*
The program will "recognize" the text on each page. When the process is complete, choose either option 1 or option 2 to edit or export the text of the document to Word for further editing.

Note: In Acrobat Pro DC, documents can be exported to spreadsheets, Microsoft PowerPoint presentations, and even images.

Working with styles in Microsoft Word

Applying styles to a document is a great way to make it look neat and consistent. Styles apply the same look (font, paragraph spacing, colour, and so on) to headings, paragraphs and sections of individual text.

In Word:

To apply a style, move the cursor to the paragraph or heading you wish to apply a style to (or highlight the text to select it), and select a style from the **Styles** group on the **Home** tab. The style is applied to the paragraph or the text you have selected.

Styles can also be modified to suit your preference.

Modify a style

If you would like to modify an existing style, choose the style you wish to edit (Normal, Title, Subtitle, and so on) by right-clicking on the style and choosing **Modify.** The **Modify Style** dialog box will open. Under the **Formatting** section, select the font, font size, alignment, spacing, and colour you wish to apply to the style. If you are happy with your selection, click **OK.**

Proofing tools

It is important to familiarise yourself with the proofing tools of your chosen word processing application. Good spelling and grammar are important in a professional environment. A document that is poorly written looks unprofessional, regardless of fancy styles and SmartArt Graphics that make it look pretty on the surface.

Note: SmartArt Graphics are diagrams that give your document a nice flow. Diagrams are useful for designing flowcharts. SmartArt Graphics are available on the **Insert** tab of Word, Excel and PowerPoint.

Selecting and reviewing your proofing preferences

In Word, select: **File > Options > Proofing.** Review the options according to your preference.

In the Proofing section, scroll down to **When correcting spelling and grammar in Word** > **Writing style**, and choose **Grammar and Style** from the dropdown list. Choose **Settings** and review the options according to your preference.

Tips for setting preferences

In the Proofing section, scroll down to **When correcting spelling and grammar** in Word, and make sure the following options are selected:

Check spelling as you type

Mark grammar errors as you type

When these options are selected, misspelled words are underlined in red, and grammar errors are underlined in blue as you type. Deselect these options if you prefer to manually check your document for errors at a later stage.

How do I manually check my document for grammar and spelling errors?

To check your document for spelling and grammar errors, select: **Review** > **Spelling and Grammar** (or press F7).

The spelling and grammar pane will open with the first potentially incorrect word or sentence. A definition of the potential error and a suggestion of ways to correct the error will also appear. Select either **Ignore** to ignore the suggestion, or **Change** to accept a proposed change.

Note: Always review the suggestion carefully. The proposed change might not be what you want, or might not work the way you thought it would. For example, proper nouns, technical terms and industry related words can potentially be marked as misspelled when they are not. If you are certain the word you typed is spelled correctly, add the word to your dictionary by right clicking on the word and selecting **Add to Dictionary**. The red underline that indicates the word is misspelled will disappear and the word will be recognised as correct from now on.

Always check that you are adding words that are spelled correctly.

Tip: At the bottom of the spelling and grammar pane you'll be able to see what proofing language Office is using. If you prefer a different proofing language, such as English (United Kingdom) or English (United States), select it from the list. The document will apply the new proofing language when re-checking the document.

Tip: Easily correct a misspelled word by right clicking on the word (underlined in red) and selecting the correct spelling option from the list. If the word is spelled correctly, but you prefer not to add it to the dictionary, select **Ignore All**. The spell check will ignore the word.

While you are editing your document, the spell check will pause. Select **Resume** to continue checking for potential errors.

When the spelling and grammar checker is not playing along
As a new receptionist you should ask your IT Department or a manager for assistance with the settings of an application. There are many options and settings that could cause a program or a feature of a program to "misbehave". If you are not comfortable editing the settings of an application, make a list of any issues and questions you have and ask for help. Your IT Department might add a custom list of features that will work for you.

If the spelling and grammar checker is not working, and you are comfortable editing the settings in Office, check the following:
On the **Review** tab, select: **Language > Set Proofing Language**.
In the dialog box, check that **Do not check spelling or grammar** is deselected (clear the box if it is selected). Select: **File > Options > Proofing**.
Under **Exceptions for**, choose the document you are currently working on. Check that the boxes are cleared for **Hide spelling errors for this document only** and **Hide grammar errors for this document only**.

If only certain words are marked by the checker, try the following:
Select: **File > Options > Proofing**. Select the AutoCorrect Options, AutoCorrect tab. Check that the options are selected according to your

preference.

Select: **File** > **Options** > **Proofing**. Under *When correcting spelling in Microsoft Office Programs*, check the settings according to your preference.

<u>Remove a word that you mistakenly added to the Word spelling checker</u>
If you have added a word to the spelling checker and need to remove it, select: **File** > **Options** > **Proofing** > **Custom Dictionaries**. Select CUSTOM.DIC (or other default dictionary), and select **Edit Word List**. The words that you have added to the dictionary will appear in alphabetical order in the dialog box. Select the word you wish to remove and select **Delete.**

<u>A note about proofing tools</u>
Never assume that a spelling and grammar checker will catch all your mistakes, know your intention, or change your sentence for the better. Unless they are very sophisticated, spell checkers do not know if you meant to say "there" or "their", and do not know if you meant to write in the active or passive voice; it is up to you to decide whether the sentence you have written is correct or not.

Note: There and *their* are homophones. To check for homophones, select **File** > **Options** > **Proofing** and mark **Frequently confused words**.

Despite this, always use the spelling and grammar checker before you send out a document because it gives you the opportunity of having a second look. There could be a spelling mistake that you missed or an obvious grammar issue that you did not see before the document was checked for errors. Sometimes the suggestion the checker provides gives your sentence a nice flow. You have the power to accept or to ignore the suggestions.

Synonyms and Thesaurus
Synonyms and Thesaurus are very useful features that come with most

word processing applications. In Word, right-click on any word and select **Synonyms.** A list of synonyms (words that have a similar meaning) will appear if any are available for your selected word. Alternatively, choose **Thesaurus** from the dropdown on the **Review** tab.

Try it out

Let's say you want to convey that someone has put in a lot of effort on a project, but you cannot think of a word other than "work", so you write, "Joe has put in a lot of work."

On the **Review** tab, select **Thesaurus,** type "work" in the search field of the thesaurus pane, and press enter.

A list of words with a similar meaning to "work" will appear. Look for "effort" in the list.

Now write, "Joe has put in a lot of effort." The new sentence sounds nicer, but it could still be better.

Let's look for a new word for "a lot".

The thesaurus suggests "a great deal".

Now write, "Joe has put in a great deal of effort." Do you agree that this sentence sounds better than "Joe has put in a lot of work"?

Note: Do not use a random or bigger word without knowing the true meaning of the word. Synonyms have a *similar* meaning, not exactly the same meaning, as your original word. In a business environment clear communication is key, so write in a way that communicates your ideas clearly.

Track Changes

Track Changes tracks and marks any changes to a document. It indicates both what was changed and who changed what.

To edit the options for Track Changes, select the **Review** tab, and the dialog box launcher (the tiny arrow that looks like it is in a square) on the **Tracking** group. The **Change Tracking Options** dialog box will open. Choose what changes to show on the document, or select **Advanced Options** to edit additional preferences.

Note: In **Change Tracking Options**, you can select to change your username. Your username is important because it appears on any notes you add to a document. If your username is unclear or incorrect (for example, a random name, someone else's name or a misspelled name) edit it here:
Review > Change Tracking Options > Change User Name
File > Options > General > Personalize your copy of Microsoft Office

Tip: Use a professional version of your name if you are not using your full name. Don't use a name like ReceptionGirl.

To start tracking changes on a document, select: **Review > Track Changes**. Any change made to the document will be marked from now on.
To stop tracking changes, select **Track Changes** on the **Review** tab again. Any further changes will not be marked.

Choose how you would like to see changes in a document
On the Tracking group, choose to view: **All Markup, Simple Markup, No Markup or Original.**
All Markup: Shows all changes made to the document itself (deleted words have a strikethrough and additions to the document are underlined).
Simple Markup: Shows a small red line in the margin where a change has been made.
No Markup: No changes are shown (this is a preview of what your document will look like if all the changes are accepted).
Original: View the original document.

Accept and Reject changes
Changes to a document can be either accepted or rejected. To accept a proposed change, right-click on the word, sentence or paragraph that is marked and choose **Accept Insertion** (or **Accept Change** depending on the version of Office you are using). The markup will disappear and the change will be applied.
To reject a proposed change, right-click on the word, sentence or paragraph that is marked and choose **Reject Insertion**. The proposed change will be

ignored and the original text will be displayed.

View multiple changes at once

On the tracking group of the **Review** tab, select **Reviewing Pane**. All the changes made to your document will appear in a list on the revisions pane.

Adding Comments to a document

Comments allow a user to make a comment without actually editing any text. A comment is useful when a question arises, or when comments about the text need to be noted. All comments are marked with a user name (the person who is making the comment.)

Add a comment

Highlight the text you wish to comment on and select **Review** > **New Comment**. Type your comment in the box. The time the comment was made is displayed next to the user name.

Remove a comment

Right-click on the comment box and select **Delete Comment**. You can also select **Mark Comment Done** if you prefer. In later versions of Office, choose **Resolve Comment** to resolve the comment.

Reply to a comment

To reply to a comment, right-click on the comment and select **Reply to Comment.**

Text highlight colour

The second way to note changes on a document is to use the **Text Highlight Color** on the **Home** tab. If you have edited or wish to point out a section of a document (and it is not necessary to keep a record of the original text), highlight what you have changed in a colour. This is a simple way to draw attention to certain sections of a document. The highlight can easily be removed by selecting the text that has been highlighted and choosing **No Color** from the **Text Highlight Color** function.

Using the Find tool

As a receptionist you might come across a word or a name that has been misspelled throughout an entire document. Do not waste time reading pages of text when you can search for the word and easily replace it from the Home tab: **Home > Replace (Replace** appears on the **Editing** group of the ribbon), or press Ctrl+F to begin the search.

Use **Find** on the **Home** tab to quickly find a word you are looking for. Every appearance of the word will appear in a list in the navigation pane (the navigation pane usually appears on the left, but it can be moved to another location on the screen). The number of results will appear at the top of the list. Scroll down to the sections you wish to jump to.

If you choose **Replace** on the **Home** tab, a dialog box with three options opens: **Find, Replace** and **Go To.**

Use **Find** to quickly find a word you are looking for. Every instance of the word will be highlighted as you select **Find Next**.

Use **Replace** to replace a word.

In the **Find what** field, type the word or phrase you wish to replace (the incorrect word or phrase). In the **Replace with** field, type the word or phrase that must appear (the correct word or phrase). The document will jump to each instance of the word or phrase. Select **Find Next** to jump to all the instances of the word or phrase you wish to replace. If you are happy that an individual instance should be replaced, choose **Replace.** If you are confident that all the instances of the word must be replaced, choose **Replace All**. Only use **Replace All** if you do not wish to view each instance of the word before replacing it.

Undo Typing

If you have made an error, before saving your changes, choose **Undo Typing** or press Ctrl+Z.

The **Undo Typing** function appears in the Quick Access Toolbar.

The option to undo your last action works in succession. This means that it steps back in sequence. For instance, if you type **A** then **B** then **C**, each instance of Ctrl+Z or click on the **Undo** command in the Quick Access

Toolbar, will undo one action in sequence backwards, which means that it will undo the **C** then the **B** then the **A.**

Finding a document or file that is missing

If you cannot remember where you saved a document you have been working on in Word (Excel and PowerPoint have the same function), select: **File > Open > Recent** (or **File > Open Recent** depending on the version of Office you are using). A list of recent documents is displayed.

In certain versions of Office, the document location appears underneath the document name. If your document is not in the list, scroll down and select **Recover Unsaved Documents**. Any unsaved files will appear in the file location. However, there is no guarantee that the file recovered from **Unsaved Files** is your complete document, or will be there at all. Make sure you save your documents to a location you will remember.

Working with templates

If you are working on a template, or a previous version of a document that you wish to keep, use the **Save As** function to save the document with a different name **before** you start editing.

Document recovery

If the AutoSave or AutoRecover function is turned on (ask your IT Department to assist you with AutoSave in Office 365 and AutoRecover in Office 2019), Office will attempt to recover documents lost when the computer (or application) crashed or turned off unexpectedly.

To recover an earlier version of your document, select: **File > Manage Document.**

A list of autosaved documents and the time the autosave was applied will appear beneath **Manage Document.** If you select a document from the autosave list, you have an opportunity to compare the changes with the document version you are currently working on, or to restore to an earlier version.

Tip: Nothing works better than Save; save documents you are working on as often as possible.

Comparing documents

Comparing documents is a very useful feature. Documents with the same name or the same content are passed around the office, or are worked on from different locations (the same copy of a document could be saved locally on your computer, on a removable disk (USB flash drive) or on the shared network drive). After a while it might not be clear which document has the correct content.

To view two documents side by side, open the two documents you wish to compare and select: **View** > **View Side by Side**. The documents will appear side by side in separate windows.

To scroll each window independently, deselect: **View** > **Synchronous Scrolling**. When selected, synchronous scrolling will scroll the pages of both windows simultaneously.

Note: Never edit original files. Instead, use the **Save As** option in your chosen application to save a copy of the file to work on. If you are unable to undo a big mess, simply discard the file and retrieve the original, save a copy of it and start again.

Marking documents with watermarks

When a document is near completion it is easy to mistake it for the final version. Mark documents that are still in progress with a watermark that says **Draft**; this avoids mistaking the working copy for the final version.

To add a watermark to a document, select the **Design** tab and choose **Watermark** > **Custom Watermark**. The Printed Watermark dialog box will open. Select Text Watermark and type DRAFT in the Text field and click OK or Apply.

A watermark that says "DRAFT" will be displayed on the pages of the document. If the watermark is too dark or too large, select a lighter colour or a different font on the Printed Watermark dialog box.

Similarly, a CONFIDENTIAL, ASAP, DO NOT COPY, or any other watermark you choose can be added to your document. To view additional watermarks, select **More Watermarks from Office.com** on the **Design** tab > **Watermark** dropdown list.

Microsoft Outlook

Microsoft Outlook is an email application that also includes other useful functions like a calendar, to do list, and reminders.

Before we jump into Outlook's additional functions, let's have a look at Outlook as an email application.

Compose a new email

In Outlook, to compose a new email select: **Home > New Email**.

In the **To** field, type the email address of the recipient. Separate more than one recipient with a semi-colon (;).

For example, joe@thehannasmithagency.com; jane@thehannasmithagency.com (these are fictitious email addresses).

If your company has an address book, select **To...** and select the user or group you wish to send the email to.

Add users or groups to the **Cc** or **Bcc** field if applicable. (See Chapter four, *The address bar*.)

In the **Subject** field, type the subject of your email.

In the body, type the message you wish to send.

When you are ready to send the message to the recipient(s), select **Send**.

Save a draft copy of your email message

If you are composing an email that you wish to send at a later time (you are getting a head start on an email you know will take a long time to write), save a copy using the **Save** command on the Quick Access Toolbar, or by selecting **File > Save.**

A copy of the email will appear under **Drafts.**

When you are ready to send, select **Send.**

Tip: Do not type the recipient's email address in the **To, Cc** or **Bcc** fields before you are ready to send the email. If you accidently hit **Send** instead of **Save** while drafting an email, the recipient will receive your half-written draft.

Inserting an attachment
An attachment is a file that accompanies and "attaches to" the email message.

Tip: Do not send large files as attachments. Email is not designed to transfer large files, and many email providers apply a limit to the size of attachments that may pass through their servers. If your email exceeds the allowable limit (the limit will vary depending on your email provider and the rules for sending attachments applied by your company or the recipient's provider or company), you will most likely receive an error message of some sort. Contact your IT Department if you receive a message that your email was not delivered or exceeded the maximum size limit.
If you need to send files that exceed the allowable limit set by the email provider(s), try an online file transfer solution like WeTransfer. WeTransfer allows a user to send files up to 2 GB for free.

Note: Limits can also be placed on the types of files you are sending. For example, certain file extensions, such as .exe files (this indicates a file that contains a program), are blocked by email providers because they are considered potential virus threats.

To insert a file as an attachment, open a **New Email** and select: **Insert >
Attach File** > *Browse to select the file you wish to insert* > **Insert.**
Alternatively, insert a document you have recently edited by selecting **Insert > Attach File**, and choosing it from the list.

Inserting an outlook item

If you would like to attach another email (or a number of emails) to your new email message, you can do so by selecting **Insert > Outlook Item**.

From the list, select the folder that contains the email message (such as the Inbox or Sent items), and select the email from the list. On the **Insert As** option, choose to insert the email either as an attachment, or as text into the body of your email. Select **OK.**

Viewing emails in a certain order

Outlook allows you to view and arrange your emails in almost any way you choose.

The commands on the **Arrangement** group of the **View** tab are designed to give you complete control over your view. This section will focus on the most useful options.

View by **Date**

Viewing emails by date, and from newest to oldest, makes it less likely that you will miss emails as they come in.

On the **View** tab, select **Date > Reverse Sort**.

Reverse Sort changes the sorting order between newest and oldest, and vice versa.

View by **From** and **To**

The **From** and **To** commands on the **Arrangement** section group all email messages based on who sent emails to you, and who emails were sent to. This is useful if you are searching for an email from a specific recipient or sender. Outlook will sort the emails alphabetically according to the recipient or sender's name.

View by **Importance**

This option is useful when you are looking for an email that was marked as important, or if you want to check whether you have forgotten to give attention to an important email. If you select to view emails by importance, all emails marked important will be grouped together.

<u>View by **Flag: Due Date** and **Flag: Start Date**</u>

Viewing emails by Flag is useful when you do not want to miss the start date or due date for a project or any instruction that was noted in the corresponding email message.

> *Tip:* In the morning, set your view to Flag: Due Date and Flag: Start Date to check you have not missed the start or due date for a project!

Using flags

Flags are a convenient way to apply reminders and due dates to email messages. Flagging creates a **To Do** item that can be viewed on the **View** tab > **To-Do Bar** > **Tasks** list.

Let's say you received an email from the head of the Human Resources Department to book a table at a specific restaurant in three weeks' time. The restaurant does not take bookings more than one week in advance, so how do you remind yourself to take action on this email on a specific date?

On the **Home** tab, select **Follow Up** and choose **Add Reminder** from the dropdown list.

Set the **Flag to** field to the action you should take. In this case, set the action to **Read,** and set the date to the Monday of the week the restaurant will take your reservation. Set the time to 08:00 or to when the restaurant opens that morning. Select **OK.**

Outlook Tasks and Reminders

In addition to being an application for drafting and exchanging emails, Outlook has some handy features for the new receptionist. Tasks and reminders help with time management, and ensure that tasks receive attention in a timely fashion. Tasks can be set at low, normal or high priority, percentage of completion, and status. The status of a task indicates whether the task has started, is in progress, completed, waiting on someone else, or deferred.

Figure 2

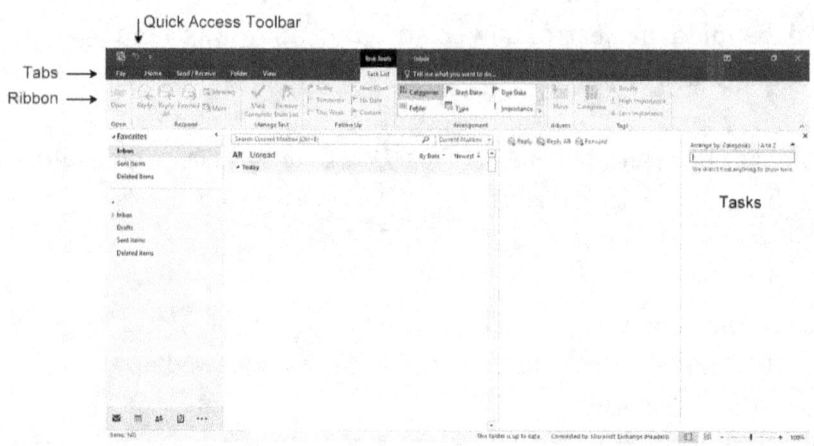

Creating a new task

In Outlook, select: **View > To-Do Bar > Tasks.**

The **To-Do Bar** will open. Type in the name of a task (such as Print proposal for Marketing Department) in the **Type a new task** field and press enter. Repeat to add new tasks.

Setting the status, priority and reminders for tasks

All tasks are different; some are simply reminders to keep you on track with daily duties and ad hoc activities, while other tasks are important and have strict deadlines. To set the priority level of a task double click on the task to open it.

Enter a **Start Date** and a **Due Date**. The start date indicates when the task will begin, and the due date indicates when the task must be complete.

Set the **Status** of the task. The status will change as you progress with the task.

Set the **Priority** of the task; this allows you to prioritise your work. Prioritisation helps with time management and prevents you from spending too much time on low priority tasks.

Set the percentage of completion (**% Completion**). This is a handy field because it shows how far a task is before it is due.

Tip: Always update the **Status** and **% Complete** as the task progresses.

Set a **Reminder** for the task by selecting the checkbox. Enter a date and time for the reminder to pop up.

Tip: Give yourself enough time to complete tasks; do not set a reminder for fifteen minutes before a task is due if you know it will take you two hours to complete that task.

Additional settings

Open a task from the task pane by selecting the task and choosing **Open**, or double-clicking on the task.

On the ribbon you'll find a variety of options for managing tasks. Mark tasks that are complete by selecting **Mark Complete**, or assign tasks to users or groups by selecting **Assign Task**. Set recurrent tasks by selecting **Recurrence**, set a time for following up by selecting **Follow Up**, and even **Categorize** tasks by colour.

If a manager requires status reports on tasks, send a report from the task by selecting **Send Status Report**. A report that contains the details of the task, such as the start and end date, status, and % complete will populate in a new email message.

Make sure to save any changes by selecting **Save & Close**.

To delete a task, select **Delete.**

Making images smaller

Images can be a hassle to work with in emails and documents. More often than not, images are far too large to be attached to emails or to be inserted into documents or the body of an email. Knowing how to quickly reduce the size of an image could save you a lot of time and frustration.

Using Microsoft Paint

Microsoft Paint is a simple graphics editor that comes with all versions of Windows.

Open Microsoft Paint, and select **File > Open.** Browse to the location of the image you wish to edit and select **Open.** The image will open.

Select **Resize** on the ribbon. Make sure the **Maintain aspect ratio** checkbox is selected.

Reduce the size of the image by a **percentage** or by **pixels.**

If you choose percentage, type the percentage by which the image must be reduced and click **OK.** For example, if the image must be half the size, type 50 in the horizontal field; the vertical field will adjust automatically if **Maintain aspect ratio** is checked. If the image must be 30 percent of the current size, type 30.

The image will be reduced to the percentage you have chosen. Select **File > Save As** to save a copy of the smaller image. Never replace the original image because you might need a bigger version for something else at a later stage.

If an image must be a certain number of pixels, choose to reduce the size by pixels.

Make sure that **Maintain aspect ratio** is checked. Type in the required number of pixels and press **OK.** The image will be reduced to the number of pixels you have entered.

Note: The quality of your image will be reduced if you make it bigger than it was originally.

Sending marketing and other copy to a professional printer

Never be too pressured by a deadline to check a proof copy of material for print. When you send a file to a printer, the printer will send a proof copy back to you for approval before anything actually goes to print. Even if you have checked the document that you sent to the printer one hundred times, the final proof copy is the most important to check because there could be a subtle variation to the file you sent that is not acceptable to the company, for example, a colour variation or blurry company logo. The reason your material could look slightly different is that digital files go through a process at the printer that changes the format of the original file. Always check that any variation from your original file is acceptable to the company.

General IT security tips

Follow the rules and guidelines of your company's IT policy. If your company does not have an IT policy or the IT policy does not cover general IT security, here are a few tips for keeping your data secure:

· Do not use a random removable disk (USB flash drive) that is lying around the office. Ask your IT Department to investigate what is on it before you plug it in to your computer because the disk could contain a computer virus.

· Always check that your antivirus program is running and up to date. Report any failed updates to your IT Department or let them know if you do not have a working antivirus program.

· Do not install software from the internet. Ask your IT Department to install the programs you need.

· Never give anyone access – remote or local – to your computer unless you are authorized to do so.

· Never give out your password unless you are authorized to do so.

· Learn to recognise phishing scams. Trends in phishing scams include links in an email to "update login details" or "confirm credentials" of online accounts. These scams are intended to trick you into providing scammers with sensitive information (usernames, passwords, and banking details). Other trends of online scams include generic greetings (addressing you as Dear Friend or Dear User), poor grammar and spelling, and emails that warn of account termination of some kind. If you suspect you are being scammed, contact your IT Department or a manager. Do not click on links in an email you suspect is a scam or use the contact information in the suspicious email for inquiries.

· Attend user awareness training. Companies sometimes offer their staff training on identifying scams and viruses. Attend as many security workshops as possible to broaden your knowledge of IT security.

· If you have not explicitly requested IT assistance be cautious when dealing with individuals who claim they have been sent to work on your computer. Ask a manager or your IT Department if they have authorized individuals from outside the company to work on your computer/printers/cables/phones before allowing them access to your work space. Your manager will appreciate your diligence.

Terms and Definitions

Application software: A software program that allows a user to perform a task. Microsoft Word is a word processing application.

Cloud-based service: A service that runs in the cloud. The cloud is a term used for applications or storage solutions that are accessed from your computer, but are installed on servers that sit elsewhere.

Proof copy: A copy of a document that shows how the final product will look when it is printed. A proof is sent to a client for final approval.

Operating system (OS): Applications are run on an operating system; Windows® is an operating system.

Computer virus: Malicious software.

Flowchart: A visual representation of a process.

IT Policy: There are many kinds of IT policies, but generally IT policies describe the appropriate use of and approach to security of the company's computer systems, facilities, networks, hardware, software applications and the internet.

Chapter eight

POPI, the GDPR, and the receptionist

Issues regarding the privacy and security of our personal information have been highlighted in recent years. Social media platforms, companies involved with direct marketing and public as well as private bodies that process sensitive information are amongst those which may no longer collect, use, share and store personal information irresponsibly. In fact, non-compliance with data protection laws can lead to hefty fines and even imprisonment. This section provides a basic overview of data protection laws for information and guidance purposes only. This information does not constitute legal advice and it should be kept in mind that each individual set of facts should be considered on the basis of its own merits. This chapter is included to provide the new receptionist with a starting point to understand the significance of dealing with personal information in the context of an office environment.

Summary of what is included in this section:
- **Background and application: POPI and the GDPR**
- **Let's recap in simpler terms**
- **POPI and the reception desk**

Note: This section contains a lot of legal terminology. If you are not interested in the nuts and bolts of POPI, skip to the sections *Let's recap in simpler terms* and *POPI and the reception desk.*

Background and application: POPI and the GDPR

The European Union is considered to be the front runner when it comes to the promulgation (when a new law is announced) of data protection laws, and therefore provides a base for the extension of the right to protection of personal information to other countries. In South Africa, the Protection of

Personal Information Act 4 of 2013 (**"POPI"**) was signed into law on 19 November 2013 and draws extensively from the predecessor of the European Union's General Data Protection Regulations (**"GDPR"**) which came into play on 25 May 2018 and applies to all European Union countries, namely the European Union's Data Protection Directive known as Directive 95/46/EC (**"EU Directive"**).

Are POPI and the GDPR similar?

The principles and conditions of POPI and the GDPR are similar in many ways as both of these laws aim to be consistent with the intended international position regarding information and data protection. Another reason for their similarity is that POPI draws extensively from the EU Directive (the predecessor of the GDPR) and on comparison one will find that the foundational principles and the purposes of the respective laws are similar. The differences are mostly with regard to the naming of conventions and definitions. For example, the "responsible party" in terms of POPI is referred to as the "controller" or "processor" in the GDPR, and POPI refers to "personal information", whereas the GDPR refers to "personal data".

What is POPI all about?

POPI prescribes a set of conditions and principles that regulate the collection, processing and use of personal information, and ensures the lawfulness of such actions. These principles and conditions have been enacted (made to law) to promote the constitutional right to privacy contained in section 14 of the South African Constitution and to protect a person's personal information and the use of this information by third parties. Bear in mind that different countries have their own unique privacy laws.

Importantly, POPI protects persons from suffering damage and harm by requiring entities and parties who receive their personal details to protect the confidentiality and integrity of such information. POPI therefore places an important responsibility on parties who collect, store, use and destroy personal information, and also provides rights and solutions to persons whose rights have been infringed in terms of POPI. It requires the relevant parties dealing with personal information to take care of such information and protects the general public against the incorrect and unauthorised use of their personal information, whether used for purposes of identity theft, abusive marketing practices or other unauthorised purposes. It is important to be aware that POPI does not aim to stop the flow or sharing of personal information, but rather aims to establish and set guidelines and rules for how this must be done in line with international standards, to protect the privacy of the persons whose personal information is being processed.

In a nutshell, it all comes down to how organisations and businesses may handle the personal information of their clients and customers, and a person's control over their own personal information. For example, you the individual now have the right to ask what personal information a company has about you on its records, to correct incorrect information, and to have the information deleted. Businesses that process personal information are now accountable for the processing of such personal information and are required to have data protection policies in place, to inform individuals for what purpose their data is being collected, for how long the data will be stored, and so on.

Who is the responsible party?
The responsible party is the individual or company, either public or private, that processes personal information and determines its purpose. The responsible party is, for example, a company or agency that processes the data of its employees and clients. A responsible party should not be confused with an operator who is a person processing the information on the instruction of the responsible party by contract or mandate, and is not under the direct authority of the responsible party. When personal information is processed by an operator the responsible party still remains responsible for the processing.

What is personal information as contemplated in POPI?
In terms of POPI, personal information is any information relating to an identifiable, living natural person and, if applicable, to an existing

identifiable juristic person (which is known as a "data subject").

Personal information may therefore include, but is not limited to any of the following – information relating to race, gender, sexual orientation, medical history, criminal history, religion, beliefs, disabilities, marital status, pregnancy, language, education, finances, employment history, online identifiers, pseudonyms, physical address, telephone numbers, and biometric information. If processing a name of a person reveals that person's personal information, then the name is also considered personal information.

What is special personal information as contemplated in POPI?

It is important to note that certain sensitive categories of personal information amount to special personal information, and those categories have even stricter requirements when it comes to the collection, processing, use and deletion or destruction thereof. Special personal information may include information concerning a child and personal information concerning religious or philosophical beliefs, race or ethnic origin, trade union membership, political persuasion, health, sexual life or criminal behaviour, and may not be processed without the necessary authorisation and consent of the data subject.

An authorised party may, however, process special personal information if the necessary consent has been obtained from the data subject, and the requirements set in terms of part B of POPI have been met.

POPI does however, stipulate certain circumstances when the prohibition on the processing of special personal information does not apply and specific authorisation therefore shall not be necessary.

What is the processing of personal information as contemplated in POPI?

The processing of personal information involves any collection, use, storage, deletion or destruction of personal information. The processing of personal information is of an ongoing nature and compliance with the provisions of POPI must be in place for as long as the personal information is being processed (which includes the storage thereof).

What is lawful processing?

POPI makes provision for eight conditions which govern the lawful processing of personal information. These so-called pillars of compliance must be adhered to by responsible parties in order to ensure that they successfully perform their obligations in terms of POPI and lawfully process personal information. These are discussed in more detail below:

Condition 1: Accountability

Responsible parties carry the obligation of ensuring that personal information is processed lawfully and that the conditions to ensure such lawful processing are complied with. POPI makes responsible parties accountable for their processing activities and sets out their liability in the event that personal information is not processed in a lawful manner.

Condition 2: Processing limitation

This POPI compliance pillar is founded on the basis that personal information should be processed lawfully; that there should only be a minimal processing of personal information; that the consent of data subjects should be obtained; that there must be justification by responsible parties for their processing of personal information; and that personal information must be, as far as is reasonably practicable, collected directly from the particular data subject.

Personal information may only be processed if such processing is adequate, relevant and not excessive. Thus, the nature and scope of the processing activity must be clear.

Condition 3: Purpose specification

POPI requires that personal information must be collected for a specific, explicitly defined and lawful purpose related to a function or activity of the responsible party. Data subjects should also be aware of such processing and the purpose thereof.

Condition 4: Further processing limitation

In terms of POPI any further processing of personal information must be in accordance or compatible with the purpose for which the personal information was originally collected. This original purpose must not be deviated from during the course of the processing of personal information.

Condition 5: Information quality

Data quality is a significant aspect to be considered since data that is of a sub-standard quality may negatively affect a data subject. Data quality is also important when it is considered that personal information generally carries commercial value.

POPI obliges responsible parties to take reasonably practicable steps to ensure that all the personal information which they collect is complete, accurate and not misleading. Responsible parties also carry the obligation of ensuring that personal information is updated if the circumstances so require.

Condition 6: Openness

A cornerstone of POPI is the promotion of transparency. This goal is advanced through the condition of "openness" which, in essence, requires that data subjects must be notified when their personal information is being processed. Simply put, this means that information should not be processed in secret. Records must also be kept by responsible parties of all processing activities conducted by them.

Condition 7: Security safeguards

The use of the word "protection" in the title of POPI places emphasis on securing personal information and an obligation to ensure that it remains safe. Ensuring the security of personal information of data subjects is the most important condition for lawful processing in terms of POPI, since security failures and breaches have the potential for data subjects to suffer significant harm. POPI obliges responsible parties to ensure the integrity and confidentiality of personal information in their possession. In advancing data protection, responsible parties must take into account generally accepted information security practices and procedures that it may put in place, as well as practices and procedures that may be required by it in terms of industry specific rules and regulations. There is accordingly not a "one size fits all" approach when it comes to personal information, and security measures will have to be designed and organised in accordance with the nature and business practices of a particular responsible party, the types of personal information which they process and the potential harm that may emanate from a security breach.

Condition 8: Data subject participation

Data subjects are entitled, in terms of POPI, to request access to the personal information held by a responsible party, as well as the amendment and deletion of such information.

Responsible parties will be obliged, if so requested, to provide confirmation (free of charge) to data subjects that they hold their personal information, to provide a description of the personal information in question and to confirm the identity of all third parties or the categories of third parties who have received their personal information.

What is an information officer?

An information officer refers to the individual within the relevant entity or institution that is a responsible party in terms of POPI, who will predominantly be responsible for ensuring compliance with POPI and being responsible for the governance, management and security of personal information. All responsible parties are obliged in terms of POPI to identify an information officer.

Let's recap in simpler terms

Are POPI and the GDPR similar?

Yes. POPI and the GDPR are similar because they both strive to be in line with international standards on data protection and they both draw extensively from the EU Directive. POPI and the GDPR differ mostly with regard to naming conventions and definitions.

What is POPI all about?

POPI regulates how your personal information may be collected, used, stored, and destroyed by the party collecting it. POPI protects your right to privacy.

What is personal information as contemplated in POPI?
Personal information is information that can identify or is about a natural or juristic person. Personal information is information about a person's race, gender, sexual orientation, medical history, criminal history, religion, beliefs, and so on. (See a comprehensive list in the corresponding section above.)

What is special personal information as contemplated in POPI?
Special personal information is a category of personal information that is regarded as sensitive, such as information about a child or a person's sexual life or health. (See a comprehensive list in the corresponding section above.) The rules for collecting, using, storing, and destroying sensitive information are stricter.

What is the processing of personal information as contemplated in POPI?
Collecting, using, storing, and deleting or destroying personal information.

What is lawful processing?
To lawfully process personal information the responsible party must comply with eight conditions:
Condition 1: Accountability – The responsible party must ensure that the conditions for lawful processing are complied with. The responsible party is accountable for the processing of personal information.
Condition 2: Processing limitation – This condition ensures that there is a reason for collecting personal information, that there is consent from the data subject, that processing is minimal (only information that is relevant and that will actually be used should be collected) and if possible, that information is collected directly from the data subject.
Condition 3: Purpose specification – The reason for collecting personal information must be lawful and for a specific reason (for the task at hand). The data subject must be aware of the reason and that their information is

being collected.

Condition 4: Further processing limitation – Personal information may only be used for the original purpose for which it was collected. Personal information may not be kept indefinitely or for longer than needed.

Condition 5: Information quality – Personal information that is collected must be complete, accurate and not misleading. Personal information must be updated by the responsible party if necessary.

Condition 6: Openness – Processing of personal information may not be done in secret. The responsible party must keep records of processing activities.

Condition 7: Security safeguards – The responsible party must ensure that the information in its possession is secured and stays safe.

Condition 8: Data subject participation – A data subject has the right to ask whether a responsible party holds personal information on them and, if so, may request to access that information, have the information updated or deleted.

What is an information officer?

The person within an organisation that ensures compliance with POPI.

Note: The GDPR right to erasure or "right to be forgotten".

Does your company have a visitor check-in book? Do you receive clients who reside in the EU or do you reside in the EU and receive clients at reception? If so, you need to comply with the GDPR's provisions for consent and right to be forgotten for the data subject. According to De Cooman (2017), "Under the new regulations, consent must be freely given, specific, informed and unambiguous to meet GDPR requirements." If a data subject withdraws their consent or objects to their information being processed, or information is no longer needed, their data must be deleted without delay by the controller. To help manage this, your visitor management system must be GDPR compliant.

Read the blog post, "Managing visitors to your business – balancing a warm corporate welcome and GDPR" on GDPR Report: https://gdpr.report/news/2017/12/22/managing-visitors-business-balancing-warm-corporate-welcome-gdpr/.

POPI and the reception desk

As a receptionist you may have access to the personal information of colleagues, business partners, and clients. Personal information, and especially special personal information, must be processed lawfully in accordance with the conditions as set out above. Let's look at a few questions a receptionist may have regarding the lawful processing of personal information:

Q: I have authorised access to a program that shows me a list of clients' birth dates. May I compile a birthday list from this information so that the company can email or call each client on their birthday?

A: No, you may not. POPI regards authorised access to personal information as possession of that information. If you are in possession of personal information you are regarded as the responsible party with regard to the processing of that personal information. If the client did not initially give consent for the processing of his or her personal information for the purpose of receiving a birthday email or telephone call, the information may not be processed for this purpose.

Q: I have been asked to set up a form and to send it around the office to get each staff member's birth date so that a manager can send them a message on their birthday each year. May I collect this information?

A: Yes, as long as each employee knows exactly why they are filling in the form. The purpose for the collection of the personal information must be specified on the form, and provision must be made for the employees to agree to be contacted on their birthday. If an employee wishes to remove their name from the list for any reason or correct the information, they must be allowed to do so. The form must be secured at all times.

Q: A colleague is on maternity leave and a client has called in requesting to speak with her. May I say that she is on maternity leave?

A: As a rule in terms of POPI, no, a receptionist will not be permitted to disclose the type of leave that the employee is on. However, in most cases it's likely that the employee will consent (either in line with their employer's request or to place their absence in context to clients or customers) to the disclosure of such information. This is very context specific and should be considered on a case by case basis.

Q: I work at a company that collects information on religious denominations for research purposes. May I compile a list of persons according to their religion and send them holiday related messages?
A: No, you may not. The persons did not initially consent to providing their information for the purpose of receiving a holiday related message. Their information may therefore not be processed for this purpose.

Q: I was asked to send out an invitation to clients from a list that my manager set up. To save time, I copied all the email addresses into the Cc field and sent the email. The sent email now displays the email address of each person to all the recipients. What must I do?
A: Any personal information that can identify a living natural person is considered to be personal information in terms of POPI. Even email addresses that display different variations of a person's name (pseudonyms) are prohibited if that can identify the person. And again, those persons have not consented to having their data shared. Contact a manager immediately and inform them that you have sent out this information.

Tip: Use the Bcc (Blind Carbon Copy) field when sending emails to a group of people. The Bcc field hides the email addresses from the recipient(s).

Q: I have sent an email to the wrong person. The email contains the physical address, sick note and telephone number of an employee. What must I do?
A: POPI ensures the confidentiality of personal information in the possession of the responsible party. Report the incident to the designated Information Officer or a manager immediately.

Tip: Always check that the correct person's email address is entered into the **To, Cc** and **Bcc** fields. Many email programs predict the email address when you begin to type, and it is easy to hit enter and not realise that the email address is not that of the person you intended to contact.

Tip: When you are handling personal information be extra careful when you use the **Forward** and **Reply All** functions in your email program. If the content of the email contains any personal information do not simply forward the email along to another party if they are not permitted to receive the information.

Q: A client has called in and asked me for a copy of the personal information my company has on them. What must I do?

A: You or someone at your company will be trained to handle this query because it is not quite as simple as randomly sending information. A company is required to be open and transparent about the personal information that they are processing. You will most likely send the client a text file that contains the information they have requested as it applies to their right of access. In the event that you do not know how to handle the relevant request, ask the Information Officer for assistance.

Q: My company has a website that displays the photographs and job titles of employees. Is a photograph not personal information?

A: Yes, it is. Since a photograph can identify a natural person, it is considered personal information. If the employees have consented to their photographs being displayed on the company website then it is allowed.

Note: Can you see how important **consent** is?

General security tips: Reduce the risk of a data breach by keeping information at the reception desk safe.

Do not leave any login credentials (such as a Wi-Fi password) stuck to your computer screen with a sticky note where visitors can see the information. Login information should also not be written on a desk pad or on a piece of paper that is stuck to the desk.

Do not leave handwritten address books or files that contain personal information or confidential company information on a reception desk that receives customers or guests, or where unauthorized persons can easily access the information.

Terms and Definitions

Enact: A law is passed.

Entities and parties: Examples include individuals, companies, groups, and institutions.

Juristic person: A juristic person is not a natural person (a human person), but is recognised as a "person" with rights. A company is a juristic person.

Mandate: A commission to do something.

Principles and conditions: Rules and the specifications or terms that govern the rules.

Prohibition: When something is stopped by law. For example, a prohibition against selling cigarettes to persons under a certain age.

Promulgate: To declare something new such as a new law.

Chapter nine

You and your work

Performing well at work is not just about technical skill, it is also about planning, organisation, and attitude. This section provides tips on how to better manage your day, present your work, and advance your career.

Summary of what is included in this section:
· **Dress**
· **Your work**
· **Keep lists**
· **Doing something fast versus doing something well**
· **Manage your time**
· **Using mobile phones in the workplace**
· **Building a career**

Dress

Dress says a lot about a company. The way staff dress gives an indication of which industry they work in, and what the ideals and interests of the company are. A company's ideals and interests are called *company culture*. (See Chapter five, Terms you will come across in a business environment.)
A receptionist is often the first person people see when visiting a company. If you work at a reception desk that receives clients or guests (or executives from other branches), follow the dress code of the company.

Note: Companies might have different dress codes for different departments.

Don't lose the opportunity to meet executives and get involved in the company because of poor dress. Think about it; if you are consistently well presented, managers will gladly ask you to tag along to meetings to take the minutes or to help out because they are comfortable pointing you out as a part of their team.

Your work

The way you present your work is just as important as the way you present yourself. Make sure that your files are neat, labelled, and organised. Place loose papers in files or envelopes, and present paperwork in folders, or in sections that are labelled or secured in some way. Sticky notes, for example, are easy to write on, apply and remove. If you have proofread a hardcopy document and need to point out an error or have a question, write it on a sticky note and attach the note to the edge of the page. If you have a document that must be signed, mark the pages that need to be signed with a certain colour sticky note. For example, use colours for different purposes, such as red for a question, yellow for an error, and blue for a signature. This allows the person you are giving the document to, to focus on the sections they have time to deal with.

Keep lists

I cannot stress enough how important to-do lists are. A receptionist is the go-to person for reminders, which can be anything from appointments to tasks to birthdays. Keep a file on your computer (or a hardcopy file if you prefer) with lists of recurring appointments, important dates, events, tasks, and holidays. A digital calendar and tasks reminder can also be used for keeping track of lists.

Doing something fast versus doing something well

When you are given a task always ask what the deadline is. Deadlines allow you time to do a task well versus doing it fast to get it out of the way.

For example, if you have a day or two to find hotels in a specific area that cater for vegetarians, don't spend a few minutes on an internet search and present the results ten minutes later as your final list. Instead, request a menu from hotels in the area and ask for referrals. Allow time for the chefs or managers to get back to you. Some hotels might be willing to prepare special meals on request, while others may not. Compile a list with options and comments and present that as your final.

If, on the other hand, you have been given a task that must be completed immediately, remove any distractions (like a cell phone and incoming emails) and get the job done.

Manage your time

Getting things done in a fast paced professional environment is a skill. Learn to manage your time so that you consistently perform both daily tasks and ad hoc tasks well.

Time management tips

Good time management starts with planning.

Plan your day. If you know that the company is hosting an office event at 10:00am that you must attend, perform routine tasks well before the event starts, or after the event has ended.

Prioritise. If you need to send a long list of emails urgently, leave low priority routine tasks for later in the day. Avoid completing low priority tasks when high priority tasks are due.

Delegate. If you have been asked to provide refreshments to guests who have arrived unexpectedly, ask someone who is not busy to purchase the refreshments while you prepare, or vice versa. Do not try to do everything yourself when help is available. When help is not available, stay calm and plan.

Communicate. If you have a long list of duties, communicate any challenges with colleagues. Someone might have a solution that you did not think of.

Make decisions. Making decisions is an important part of managing your time. If you have not made a decision, the task is not done. It is also important that you do not leave decisions you should be making to others. If you are overwhelmed, communicate the challenge. Every task in the workplace needs to be completed by someone; if you do not make a decision to complete a task, someone else must do it.

Know your limitations. If you have been given a task that is completely out of your skill set, say so. You will save yourself and the person who actually knows how to do it a late night at the office.

Using mobile phones in the workplace

Unless you are required to use your personal mobile phone for work related purposes, place your phone in a secure location while you are at work. A personal mobile phone is distracting to you, other staff, and clients. If you need to use your phone for a personal reason during business hours, do so in a designated break area or during a lunch or tea break. Remember to check if your company has a mobile device policy that explains the rules for use of mobile devices at work.

Building a career

Companies both small and large often advertise internal vacancies, usually on the company's portal, website, or in a general company newsletter. Internal vacancies are designed to move staff who show an interest to the best possible place in the company for them. Promoting staff internally is good for company morale because people feel that they have a future with the company. It also reduces staff turnaround (the number of people who leave the company against the number of people who are hired in a given time) which reduces the time and cost of training new staff. Although not all positions are open for internal promotion (some positions require specific qualifications and/or experience), some positions are a good fit for someone who started out as the company's receptionist.

If you are interested in working in a particular department or in a specific position, find out if there is something you can do to make that happen in the future. The Human Resources Department will advise you on the minimum qualifications required for specific positions and the process of applying for those positions. Expressing an interest in advancement within the company is the first step to building your career.

Your attitude will play a role

Advancement is based on many factors, and one of them is your attitude. A manager might not consider you for a promotion if you have a bad attitude, especially when the new position requires you to have contact with the company's clients or to be part of a team.

Your work will play a role

The best way of determining whether you will perform the tasks of a new job well, is a review of your current performance. If you are not performing tasks efficiently, or are making excuses and handing in poor work, your chances of a promotion will be slim. On the other hand, if you perform your current tasks well, your manager will be confident in your ability to perform more demanding tasks well too.

Advancement and getting involved

Learning and experience are key to advancement. Make use of learning opportunities and get involved with as many projects as possible within your capacity. A willingness to take on more responsibility will set you apart and put you in a good position when opportunities within the company arise, especially if you have shown an interest in, or had some experience with the product or service. However, never offer to get involved if you do not have the capacity to do so successfully. Your job at reception is your first priority, so try not to take on projects at the expense of your current role.

Further learning at a university or college

Many universities and colleges offer distance learning and part-time degrees and diplomas, so perhaps you can sign up for one if you have not already done so. Choose a course or degree that will further your career or get you closer to your dream job. For example, if you are interested in working in the creative department of your company find out what qualifications you need to get there. If you do not meet the entry requirements for a particular degree, ask a counsellor at a university or college for advice. There might be a list of alternative courses that you could register for.

Terms and Definitions

Portal: A company portal is an online resource that is accessed by the company's employees for various reasons via a login. A portal can store news, training material, forms, and much more.

Inspiration

"Always be confident and optimistic. Just because you've never done something before doesn't mean you can't figure it out as easily as the next person."

Karen Kaplan – CEO of Hill Holliday (in *The Boston Globe*, 2016)

Karen Kaplan started working at the front desk of Hill Holliday in 1982; at that stage her only work experience was babysitting and waitressing. Karen was appointed CEO of the same company in 2013.

View the article, *9 lessons so anyone can go from receptionist to CEO* here: https://www.bostonglobe.com/business/2016/05/20/lessons-anyone-can-from-receptionist-ceo/hyM1sOvileHnEHJkbO0tvM/story.html.

Corrections

Although every effort has been made to ensure this book is free from errors, some mistakes may occur. If you encounter any inaccuracies in this book, please let us know; we would love to hear from you. Please report any errors to The Hanna Smith Agency at www.thehannasmithagency.com/books.

Bibliography

Preface

Stampler, L. 2013. *The Incredible Story Of Karen Kaplan's Meteoric Rise From Receptionist To CEO.* Available from: https://www.businessinsider.com/how-karen-kaplan-went-from-receptionist-to-ceo-2013-5?IR=T. [19 October 2018].

Page, B. 2016. *Tributes paid to agent David Miller.* Available from: https://www.thebookseller.com/news/david-miller-dies-456991. [3 January 2019].

Chapter two

DHL. 2018. Available from: https://www.logistics.dhl/za-en/home.html. [12 December 2018].

Emirates. 2018. Available from: https://www.emirates.com/za/english/. [10 December 2018].

Time and Date AS. 1995-2018. *Daylight Saving Time – DST – Summer Time.* Available from: https://www.timeanddate.com/time/dst/. [18 December 2018].

Time and Date AS. 1995-2018. *Time Zone Abbreviations – Worldwide List.* Available from: https://www.timeanddate.com/time/zones/. [9 October 2018].

Time and Date AS. 1995-2018. *UTC – The World's Time Standard.* Available from: https://www.timeanddate.com/time/aboututc.html. [9 October 2018].

Chapter four

Cullen, M. 2018. *Business Email Salutations to a Group [Updated 2018]*. Available from: https://www.instructionalsolutions.com/blog/email-salutations-to-group. [29 November 2018].

English Oxford Living Dictionaries. 2019. pp. Available from: https://en.oxforddictionaries.com/definition/pp. [16 November 2018].

Practicing Workplace English. 2008. Pretoria: University of South Africa.

University of Sussex. 1997-2019. *Abbreviations*. Available from: http://www.sussex.ac.uk/informatics/punctuation/capsandabbr/abbr. [16 November 2018].

Chapter five

Duke, L., Fynn, H., Huxtable, B., Kamala, P., McKinlay, J., Rieger, F. & van Nieuwenhuizen, P. 2015. *Entrepreneurship 2*. Cape Town: EDGE Learning Media (Pty) Ltd.

European Commission. n.d. *What is an SME?* Available from: http://ec.europa.eu/growth/smes/business-friendly-environment/sme-definition_en. [25 November 2018].

Fortune. 2018. Available from: http://fortune.com. [11 January 2019].

Michalsons. 2016. *The Difference between Appendices, Annexures and Schedules*. Available from: https://www.michalsons.com/blog/of-appendices-annexures-and-schedules/11774. [30 January 2019].

The Banking Association South Africa. 2019. *SME Definition*. Available from: https://www.banking.org.za/what-we-do/sme/sme-definition. [7 February 2019].

Chapter six

Duke, L., Fynn, H., Huxtable, B., Kamala, P., McKinlay, J., Rieger, F. & van Nieuwenhuizen, P. 2015. *Entrepreneurship 2.* Cape Town: EDGE Learning Media (Pty) Ltd.

Chapter seven

Adobe. 2019. PDF. *Three letters that changed the world.* Available from: https://acrobat.adobe.com/za/en/acrobat/about-adobe-pdf.html. [22 November 2018].

Dummies. n.d. *WHAT'S NEW IN WORD 2019?* Available from: https://www.dummies.com/software/microsoft-office/word/whats-new-in-word-2019/. [20 December 2018].

Microsoft Support. 2018. *Frequently asked questions about grammar proofing in Word.* Available from: https://support.microsoft.com/en-za/help/290943/frequently-asked-questions-about-grammar-proofing-in-word. [20 December 2018].

UNESCO. 2018. Available from: https://en.unesco.org. [11 January 2019].

Chapter eight

Burns, Y. & Burger-Smidt, A., 2018. *A Commentary on the Protection of Personal Information Act.* Johannesburg: LexisNexis.

De Cooman, G. 2017. *Managing visitors to your business – balancing a warm corporate welcome and GDPR.* Available from: https://gdpr.report/news/2017/12/22/managing-visitors-business-balancing-warm-corporate-welcome-gdpr/. [9 February 2019].

Galetic, F. 2017. *Is your Visitor Management System GDPR-compliant? Find out with this checklist.* Available from: https://www.proxyclick.com/blog/is-your-visitor-management-system-gdpr-compliant. [8 February 2019].

Information Commissioner's Office (ico.). n.d. *Right of access.* Available from: https://ico.org.uk/for-organisations/guide-to-data-protection/guide-to-the-general-data-protection-regulation-gdpr/individual-rights/right-of-access/. [19 October 2018].

Intersoft Consulting. n.d. *Art. 17 GDPR Right to erasure ('right to be forgotten').* Available from: https://gdpr-info.eu/art-17-gdpr/. [8 February 2019].

Martinson, C. 2018. *POPI vs GDPR – IT'S COMPLICATED! Your business and international clients.* Available from: https://jjrinc.co.za/2018/02/19/popi-vs-gdpr-complicatedyour-business-international-clients/. [19 October 2018].

Michalsons. 2002-2018. *Information Officer for POPI and PAIA.* Available from: https://www.michalsons.com/focus-areas/privacy-and-data-protection/information-officer-popi-paia. [19 October 2018].

Viviers, D. 2018. *POPI and the storing of personal information.* Available from: https://www.phinc.co.za/NewsResources/NewsArticle.aspx?ArticleID=2256. [19 October 2018].

Notes

Notes

www.ingramcontent.com/pod-product-compliance
Lightning Source LLC
Chambersburg PA
CBHW071313220526
45468CB00001B/360